Youth Cultures and Poli

Socialist History 26

Rivers Oram Press
London, Sydney and Chicago

Editorial Advisers: Noreen Branson†, Eric Hobsbawm, Monty Johnstone, Victor Kiernan, David Marquand, Ben Pimlott†, Pat Thane

Editorial Enquiries: Kevin Morgan, School of Social Sciences, University of Manchester, Manchester M13 9PL or kevin.morgan@manchester.ac.uk.

Reviews Enquiries: John Callaghan, School of Humanities, Languages and Social Sciences, University of Wolverhampton, Wulfruna Street, Wolverhampton WV1 1PB or j.callaghan@wlv.ac.uk

Socialist History 26 was edited by Andrew Flinn, Matthew Worley, Kevin Morgan, Julie Johnson, Andy Croft and John Callaghan

Published in 2004
by Rivers Oram Press, an imprint of Rivers Oram Publishers Ltd
144 Hemingford Road, London, N1 1DE

Distributed in the USA by
Independent Publishers Group, Franklin Street, Chicago, IL 60610
Distributed in Australia and New Zealand by
UNIReps, University of New South Wales, Sydney, NSW 2052

Set in Garamond by NJ Design
and printed in Great Britain by T.J. International Ltd, Padstow

British Library Cataloguing in Publication Data
A catalogue record for this publication is available from the British Library
ISBN 1 85489 159 6 (pb)
ISSN 0969 4331

Contents

Notes on Contributors   **v**

Editorial   **vii**

'Learn by Doing, Teach by Being'   **1**
The children of 1968 and the Woodcraft Folk
Rich Palser

'The Hippies Now Wear Black'   **25**
Crass and the anarcho-punk movement, 1977-84
Richard Cross

The Rise and Fall of the Labour League of Youth   **45**
Michelle Webb

Memory, Youth, Hope   **59**
Features of youth activism in the last years of apartheid
Jonathan Grossman

Tributes   **83**
Noreen Branson (1910–2003)
Ben Pimlott (1945–2004)

Forum   **85**
In search of Orwell

Reviews   **100**

Books to be remembered (9)

Lytton Strachey, *Eminent Victorians* (John Saville)

Richard Steigmann-Gall, *The Holy Reich. Nazi Conceptions of Christianity, 1919–1945* (Martin Durham)

Ruan O'Donnell, *Robert Emmet and the Rebellion of 1798*; *Robert Emmet and the Rising of 1803*; Marianne Elliott, *Robert Emmet. The making of a legend* (John Newsinger)

John Callaghan, Steven Fielding and Steve Ludlam (eds), *Interpreting the Labour Party: Approaches to Labour politics and history* (Mark Phythian)

G. Lukacs, *A Defence of 'History and Class Consciousness'. Tailism and the Dialectic*, trans E. Leslie (John Callow)

Notes on Contributors

Rich Palser is a part-time research student at Oxford Brookes University, specialising in Irish labour history. His family have been active members of the Woodcraft Folk for four generations.

Richard Cross completed his doctoral study of the final years in the life of the British Communist Party in 2003. He currently co-edits the Communist History Network Newsletter http://les1.man.ac.uk/chnn

Michelle Webb is a primary school teacher in West Yorkshire. Having gained her M.A. in History, she is currently engaged on research on the Labour League of Youth at Huddersfield University. Her mother was a League member in the 1950s.

Jonathan Grossman lectures in the Department of Sociology at the University of Cape Town. His political and academic work focuses on the lived experience of the working class and processes through which working-class collectives survive and make history. He welcomes discussion around these and related issues: grossman@humanities.uct.ac.za

Editorial

Youth and youth cultures are a well-trod area, at least in sociology, cultural studies and related areas, if not so much in history and politics. In studies of the post-war emergence of teenagers with a definable youth culture separate from and a reaction against childhood and adulthood, little emphasis has been placed on the politics of youth. Indeed, one recent introduction to the changes in British society remarked on the lack of detailed work of the influence of young people in politics.[1] An obvious exception to this has the 1960s, which have come to epitomise youth politics and youthful rebellion. Many accounts of the events and the politics of that period have tended to conflate youth politics with a wider youth culture which incorporated rebellion, conflict with adult authority, spontaneity and an often confused or inchoate ideology. Eric Hobsbawm confessed that his own lack of youth hampered his understanding and writing of the history of that period.[2] Whilst elements of the assumptions about youth politics are clearly true, in the hands of historians less skilled and less willing to admit their difficulty in comprehending these developments than Hobsbawm, there is a danger that such characterisations lead to the marginalisation or trivialisation of youth movements and their politics as immature or unrealistic. This, of course, represented the attitude of some within the labour movement, not least because the challenges of youth politics were often directed against their authority as much as against more explicitly conservative forces in wider society. However, we believe that these following articles, above all else, demonstrate that in addition to their instinctive anti-authoritarianism and the spontaneous nature of many of the movements, the young people involved in the events and organisations described took their commitment to an alternative political future very seriously indeed.

The relationship of formal political parties to young people in Britain has until recently received only passing attention. Sociologist and political commentators like Mark Abrams studied young people and the Labour

Party in the late 1950s and early 1960s, and Zig Layton-Henry published articles on Conservative and Labour youth organisations in the 1970s.[3] Subsequently, there was very little work done until a new generation of historians including Laurence Black, Steve Fielding and Catherine Ellis began to show interest in Labour and its troubled relationship with 1950s and 1960s youth.[4] The history of the British Young Communist League has also been the subject of articles by Mike Waite in this journal and elsewhere, and the important role of the organisation is examined in Geoff Andrew's recent account of the last years of the Communist Party of Great Britain.[5] An international perspective on these matters is also instructive. A recent *Socialist History* article on the Dutch communist children's organisation, *Uilenspiegelclub*, invites many comparisons and contrasts with the Woodcraft Folk as described here.[6] In the articles that follow, the international flavour is to be found not only in the piece on South African youth but also in the clear sense that an internationalism, particularly when linked with an anti-war or peace campaign, was a key component of many of the movements examined here.

Whilst we assert the importance of active and politically engaged youth, we must acknowledge that these were (and are) in the minority amongst their peers. Like their adult counterparts, those youth activists who participated in political activity did so within a largely passive and often de-politicised wider society. Even in 1980s South Africa, an infinitely more politicised environment than 1950s or 1960s Britain, the politically engaged youth activists described here were a minority. So, these articles do not claim to identify some past golden era of youth activity and engagement with which to contrast the present period of passivity and apathy. Indeed, despite repeated claims regarding the indifference of young people, recent political movements in response to globalisation, the environment and the war in Iraq suggest that some young people continue to be politically active, but as in the past in campaigns of their own choosing and on their own terms. More studies of youth apathy and non-participation in labour and other struggles would be very valuable but whilst recognising the majority, we are unapologetic about offering here accounts of the activist minority.

The first article, by Rich Palser, analyses the recent history of the Woodcraft Folk. Founded in 1925, the Folk were, and indeed remain, a children's and youth organisation with close links to the co-operative movement. The organisation sought to provide an environment in which children and young adults could develop the capacity for thinking and acting for themselves within a progressive framework. Specifically the Folk hoped that the experience of collective and co-operative living whilst camping would encourage members to work towards the transformation of society. The definition of these objectives and the methods necessary to achieve them has been a contested area within the organisation, and it is this contestation that the article examines. A general history of the Woodcraft Folk has been written recently by Mary Davis[7] but Rich Palser's perceptive piece reflects on the changes wrought upon the Folk first in response to the emergence of youth culture in the 1950s and the more politicised generation of 1968, and second by the interventions of the 1968 generation, this time as parents and adult activists within the Folk in the late 1970s and early 1980s. The recent history of the Woodcraft Folk has included occasionally sharp disputes between what are sometimes referred to as modernisers and traditionalists. Palser helps to unpick the real differences which lay behind these divisions.

More than any of the others, the next article by Richard Cross deals explicitly with the difficult intersection between youth culture and youth politics. Of all the youth sub-cultures associated with the rock 'n' roll era, punk has the most openly political and aggressively rejectionist beliefs. Punk's reputation and its influence can hardly be said to have declined since 1977, rather versions of the 'myth' of punk's rebellion have continued to exert a powerful fascination for subsequent generations in Britain and elsewhere. Nevertheless, the content of punk's political ideology was and remains an extremely disputed subject. Here, Richard Cross focuses on the sometimes forgotten and historically marginalised yet influential anarcho-punk movement of which the band/collective Crass were, if not the leaders, the most prominent representatives, tracing the movement's strengths and the weaknesses which eventually undermined its influence. Deeply critical of the commercialisation and commodification of other leading punk bands, Crass and anarcho-punk sought to hold true to a concept of punk 'purity' incorporating subversion, autonomy, the DIY ethic, feminism, pacifism and the construction of an alternative society. As Cross demonstrates, Crass and their supporters were untypical of popular perceptions of punk's rejectionism and nihilism. They were politically active, especially in the peace movement of the late 1970s and early 1980s, coming into direct conflict with left- and right-wing groups also seeking a youth audience. Rather than dismissing all adult figures and past inspirations (the famous punk maxim, 'Never trust a hippy'), Crass explicitly drew on the politics of the 1960s counter-culture and hippy movement. But for all that, they were also trapped by some of the contradictions of operating within a wider youth and pop culture.

Michelle Webb is embarking on a study of Labour's League of Youth inspired in part by her mother's memories of the League in the 1950s. Using interviews and autobiographical accounts of former members, Webb focuses on the relationship between the party and its youth organisation from its early days in the 1920s until its final dissolution in 1959. The article does not concentrate on the well-known political struggles which, particularly in the 1930s, consumed the League, but rather on the different conceptions and aspirations of what a youth organisation actually entailed. The adult party viewed the League as a means of schooling young people in the ways of the party, almost as an apprenticeship. For their part, many young activists challenged the restrictions imposed on them by the party and sought greater autonomy in the control of their own affairs, as well as a more concrete role in Labour's affairs. However, focussing on conflict does not tell the whole story and Webb also stresses the comradeship that was to be found in the League's social activities, particularly in the rambling, as well as in the political education and propaganda training.

In the final article, Jonathan Grossman introduces us to the lives of young people involved in violent struggle against the brutal apartheid regime in South Africa. The article highlights the contrast between the optimism, impatience and the willingness to sacrifice their own lives that youth brought to the struggle in hope of a transformed and 'socialist' society with the failure to realise those hopes and the subsequent abandoning of that and subsequent generations of young people who fail to subscribe to the now dominant ideologies of the new South Africa. As Grossman demonstrates, for some young people involvement in the struggle led to a much more politicised view of the struggle and of the possibilities for an alternative future for South African society. Others desired a similar radical transformation of society and hence of their own lives, but without the same level of politicisation or ideological commitment they lacked the framework to cope with the failure of post-apartheid society to deliver these aspirations. For some, there is a clear sense of betrayal that their very real sacrifices have gone unrewarded in terms of the transformation of their everyday lives, and they feel increasingly marginalised and written out of the official history. However, Grossman concludes by showing how the memories and hopes of those days and the re-discovery of these collectivist struggles can play a central role in informing, renewing and sustaining those young people involved in today's campaigns and movements.

Although these articles have quite a wide-ranging subject matter there are a number of common themes about youth cultures and youth politics which arise from reading them together. Like the culture from which it emerges, youth politics often defines itself in terms of generational conflict, expressing impatience with and rejecting adult authority inside and outside the movements and struggles it associates itself with. However, this is not the whole story. While in general punk rhetorically rejected all that had gone before, Crass made reference to previous struggles and ideologies. In South Africa, some young activists explicitly venerated older workers recognising the importance of their knowledge and history and their own future position as workers. For both the League of Youth and the Woodcraft Folk, perceptions of generational conflict have to be set against the close, often familial, relations between adults and young people in these organisations.

Another contradiction of youth politics relates to the relationship with popular youth cultures. For while both punk and those movements associated with the student revolt of the 1960s emerged from and embraced elements of the youth culture of the period, they also fiercely rejected the consumerism and commodification of that culture, often in terms not dissimilar to the criticisms advanced by older voices in the labour movement. This contradiction was not easily resolved; nonetheless those young people committed to these politics were often unwavering in their rejection of the present organisation of society and the need for fundamental transformation and the creation of a better world. This characteristic enthusiasm and optimism about the need for deep-seated change, particularly when divorced from a fixed and developed ideology, can be dismissed as utopian or unrealistic, as demonstrating the typical immaturity of youth. However, we would assert that the impatience for change, the spontaneity of organisation, and the internationalism demonstrated by the youth movements described here are qualities which should be valued and embraced, as Jonathan Grossman suggests, in the struggles today.

Also in this issue, John Newsinger and Andy Croft engage in a Forum debate over the political significance of George Orwell, a subject that remains as controversial as ever despite the publication of new works about the writer and his political trajectory.

Socialist History was among the co-sponsors of a successful conference this year on the overall theme of Rethinking Social Democracy. Held at the London Institute of Historical Research over three days in April, this was the first in a series of three such conferences to be held at different venues in the UK in 2004, 2005 and 2006. A selection of papers from this first conference, which took as its specific theme Social Democracy, Culture and Society: historical perspectives, will appear in the next issue of *Socialist History*. More details about Rethinking Social Democracy, including a call for papers for the second conference, entitled The Political Economy of the Social Democracy: past, present and future, can be found at http://www.fssl.man.ac.uk/rsd.

Finally, as this issue goes to press, and thanks largely to the efforts of Richard Cross, *Socialist History* is about to launch its own website. The journal's web address is http://www.socialist-history-journal.org.uk. Comments and suggestions on this or any other aspect of the journal are welcomed by the editorial team.

Andrew Flinn
Matthew Worley

Notes

1. Abigail Beach and Richard Wright (eds.), *The Right to Belong. Citizenship and National Identity in Britain, 1930–1960* (London, 1998), p.10 cited by Catherine Ellis, 'The Younger Generation: the Labour Party and the 1959 Youth Commission', *Journal of British Studies*, 41 (2002), p.202.
2. Eric Hobsbawn, *Interesting Times* (London, 2002) pp.261–2.
3. Mark Abrams, 'The Socialist Commentary Survey' in Mark Abrams, Richard Rose and Rita Hinden, *Must Labour Lose?* (Harmondsworth, 1960), Zig Layton-Henry, 'Labour's Lost Youth', *Journal of Contemporary History*, 11 (1976), pp.275–308.
4. Laurence Black, *Old Labour, New Britain. The political culture of the Left in affluent Britain* (London, 2003), Steve Fielding, *The Labour Governments 1964–1970. Volume 1 Labour and cultural change* (Manchester, 2003), Catherine Ellis, 'The Younger Generation'.
5. Mike Waite, 'The YCL and youth culture', *Socialist History*, 6 (1994) and 'Sex 'n' Drugs 'n' Rock 'n' Roll (and Communism) in the 1960s' in Geoff Andrews, Nina Fishman and Kevin Morgan (eds), *Opening the Books* (London, 1995) and Geoff Andrews, *Endgames and New Times. The final years of British Communism 1964–1991* (London, 2004).
6. Margreet Schrevel, 'A Dutch Mix of Scouts and Pioneeers. The *Uilenspeigelclub* children, 1953–1964', *Socialist History, 21* (2002), pp.1–10.
7. Mary Davis, *Fashioning A New World* (Loughborough, 2000).

Socialist History Titles

Requests for back issues to ro@riversoram.demon.co.uk

Previous issues of *Socialist History* include:

15 Visions of the Future
...David Purdy on utopian thought; Philip Coupland on utopia in British political culture; Maureen Speller on the future in science fiction...
1 85489 115 4

16 America and the Left
...David Howell on syndicalism; Neville Kirk on American exceptionalism; Kevin Morgan on the British left and America...
1 85489 117 0

17 International Labour History
...Sheila Rowbotham on working class women's narratives; Karen Hunt on internationalism and socialist women; Paul Kelemen on Labour's Africa...
1 85489 119 7

18 Cultures and Politics
...Matthew Worley on the Third Period; Andrew Whitehead on Red London; Martin Wasserman on Kafka as industrial reformer...
1 85489 123 5

19 Life Histories
...Richard Pankhurst on Sylvia Pankhurst; Andy Croft on Randall Swingler; Malcolm Chase interviews John Saville on the *DLB*...
1 85489 129 4

20 Contested Legacies
...Mark Bevir on socialism and the state; Matt Perry on the Hunger Marches; David Renton and Martin Durham debate gender and fascism...
1 85489 135 9

21 Red Lives
...Till Kössler on West German communists; Margreet Schrevel on a Dutch communist children's club; Tauno Saarela on characters in Finnish communist magazines...
1 85489 141 3

22 Revolutions and Revolutionaries
...John Newsinger on Irish Labour; Allison Drew on experiences of the gulag; Edward Acton, Monty Johnstone, Boris Kagarlitsky, Francis King and Hillel Ticktin on the significance of 1917...
1 85489 141 3

23 Migrants and Minorities
...Shivdeep Grewal on racial politics of the National Front, Keith Copley and Cronain O'Kelly on the British Irish in Chartist times; Stephen Hipkin on rural conflict in early modern Britain...
1 85489 155 3

24 Interesting Times?
...David Howell interviews Eric Hobsbawm; John Callaghan on reviews of *Interesting Times*; Ann Hughes on Christopher Hill's work; Cambridge communists reminisce...
1 85489 157 X

25 Old Social Movements?
...Meg Allen on women, humour and the Miners' Strike; Paul Burnham on the squatters of 1946; David Young on agency and ethnicity; Charles Hobday on the Fifth Monarchy...
1 85489 158 8

'Learn by Doing, Teach by Being'
The children of 1968 and the Woodcraft Folk

Rich Palser

Looking back on the political radicalisation and ruptures of the 1960s, the historian Eric Hobsbawm identified as a key factor the rise of a specific, and extraordinarily powerful, youth culture which indicated a profound change in the relation between the generations:

> Youth, as a self-conscious group…now became an independent social agent.…The political radicalisation of the 1960s…belonged to these young people, who rejected the status of children, or even adolescents (i.e. not quite mature adults), while denying full humanity to any generation above the age of thirty, except for the occasional guru.[1]

It is with the advantage of hindsight that Hobsbawm is able to describe the self-conscious and self-confident, if not precocious, youth of the late 1960s and early 1970s whose mobilisations were in his view to shape the most dramatic political developments of that period.

In 1961, and without that advantage of hindsight, Basil Rawson was a leading member of the Woodcraft Folk. This was a voluntary organisation for children and young people which had emerged from the Boy Scout movement in the 1920s, and it regarded itself as pursuing a radically different approach to education which was neither militaristic nor jingoistic. In 1961 Rawson did not know and could not have known what would be happening less than a decade later, yet he alerted the organisation to the need to adapt its practices:

> The Folk has been well to the fore in changing and adapting educational techniques to the changes in children brought about by the impact of a changing society, but we have not been so ready (or able) to take into account the needs of the adolescent.[2]

As Rawson indicates, the Folk prided itself on its radical approach to children's education and its ability to innovate in response to their changing needs.[3] The Folk adhered to the dictum of its founding leader Leslie Paul, 'Learn by doing, Teach by being', but Rawson acknowledged that it had not always been able to do this for the adolescent youth.[4] Now that the needs of this group were shifting the Folk had to evolve to meet these changes. This article will first examine how well these adjustments prepared it for the youth radicalisation of 1968.

But perhaps more importantly it will also extend that study into the 1980s. The students whose colleges were organising centres for radical political action in the late 1960s and early 1970s subsequently became the teachers, social workers, doctors, civil servants and youth workers of the later 1970s and 1980s. The radicalism of their student days was carried into these occupations both as practitioners, and in many cases as active trade unionists. They formed a significant constituent of the 'Bennite left' that emerged in the Labour Party after 1979, and played their part in attempting to capture local authorities to radical causes. Still greater numbers than were attracted to organised socialist politics were influenced by, or found a home in, the new social protest movements that emerged as part of this radicalisation. This generation also became parents. As such they had to make decisions regarding the nurturing and education of their own children. In the 1980s some turned to the Woodcraft Folk for answers to these questions and so this article will examine not only how the Woodcraft Folk responded to the new youth culture and radicalism of 1968, but also how later in the 1980s it incorporated, and was changed by, the no-longer 'children' of 1968.

In doing so the article will build on the main published work on the history of the Folk by Mary Davis as well as suggesting a different interpretation of the organisation's more recent past.[5] Davis argues that the most important discontinuity in that history was the jettisoning of some of its previous political values in the late 1970s and early 1980s. These political values were its 'broad brush non-aligned socialism' which was expressed through its 'class conscious ideological standpoint'. She argues that whilst the Folk's most overtly political phase was during the 1930s, the Folk's 'brave stand against the cold war' shows that a clear political commitment was still present after the war. From the late 1970s onwards however these values were jettisoned 'partly through fear of losing state funding and partly because socialist politics did not fit the more mainstream agenda advocated at the time'.[6]

This interpretation is plausible, but not entirely convincing. As Davis focuses on the socialist rhetoric of the Folk rather than the actual content of its educational programme, she overstates the degree to which the Folk ever had a 'class conscious ideological standpoint' and underestimates the radical content of the turn towards the 'mainstream' of the 1980s. The radical content of this turn was the indirect result of the youth radicalisation of 1968. Although limited by space, this article will sketch the main elements of a differing interpretation to that of Davis.

The Folk and radical youth

By the late 1950s profound changes were beginning to affect young people. Writers, cultural critics, sociologists and educationalists were increasingly aware of this and tried to understand the reasons for the new 'youth culture' as it was then being dubbed. In 1960 the Albermarle Report on the Youth Service in England and Wales highlighted the fluidity of modern society in which new industries, job relocation and expanding education were increasing social mobility, and argued that:

> In such a world young people are between conflicting voices. They can sense a contradiction between what they are assured at school are this society's assumptions, and much they are invited…to admire once they leave [this] sheltered environment.[7]

The Woodcraft Folk discussed the Albermarle report and this clearly influenced Basil Rawson's 1961 proposal to experiment with new ways of working with the fourteen to seventeen-year age group.[8] Before this the age groupings of the Folk had reflected those of the school system - 'Elfin' groups for primary school children, and Pioneers for the secondary age (eleven to fifteen). At sixteen Folk members were expected to begin to play a role in running Elfin and Pioneer groups as 'helpers' and then as adult leaders:

> We have remained a children's organisation and have expected the older Pioneers to accept the same programme as put over for the younger groups and, at sixteen onwards, suddenly to take a more serious view of life and train primarily for service to the movement or the community with rapidly increasing responsibility.[9]

At the 1961 Folk conference there were reservations about the experimental youth groups getting too strong and threatening the children's groups by competing for resources. In retrospect the then general secretary, Margaret White, believes that many leaders were worried that their 'life line to the future' would be lost if Folk youth had their own groups rather than beginning their training as future Folk leaders. This fear was rein-forced by participation in the International Falcon Movement where youth organisations aligned to the social democratic parties were in her view 'top heavy', geared to creating party cadre rather than to the educational needs of children.[10] This underlying tension—whether the Folk was a children's organisation, or whether it should, and could, be an organisation for both children and youth—was to re-occur repeatedly in the coming decades. Nevertheless the experimentation went ahead, and in 1963 constitutional changes were made to establish Venturer Lodges, groups made up of the fourteen to seventeen age range.[11]

Similar attempts to discover how to cater for the youth of the new youth culture were to be found in another resolution discussed at the same con-ference:

> Whilst not wishing to change in any fundamental way the character of the Folk, we are nevertheless convinced that some aspects of our traditions are out of date and lacking in appeal to the children of today. We need new songs of our own making and our Creeds need redrafting in language more understandable to the children of this decade.

The resolution prompted considerable debate and several amendments. Supporting the resolution Peggy Aprahamian argued that the Folk needed to go on record as becoming a mass movement: 'We did not mean by a mass movement one that would lose its Folk character and identity. We meant one which was prepared to adapt itself to the times. We should be appealing to all children of the working class'. Whether by adapting to the times the organisation would lose its character and identity was a controversy that would re-emerge in subsequent debates.

What was the Folk's fundamental character which the moderniser Aprahamian was at pains to point out she did not want to undermine? Was it a 'socialist' or 'class' perspective? The Folk was formed in the mid 1920s, splitting away from the Boy Scout movement. From the beginning it was a predominantly working-class organisation. Many of its leaders were active members of their unions, the Labour Party and the Co-operative movement. The organisation saw its role as encouraging young members to become active in the labour movement when older. It also had its own 'Clause Four', the Folk Charter, which vaguely committed it to contributing to the creation of a socialist society. However in so far as it took any practical measures towards this, they consisted of the gradual education of children who would be 'fit in mind and body' and able to contribute positively to society when older. Beyond this practical activity there was little agreement on, or need for agreement on, broader questions of political perspective—hence the bitter divisions in the Folk during the Second World War between conscientious objectors and those who wanted to prosecute the 'war against fascism'. Not for nothing did Rawson say in 1949 that 'our literature, charter etc ties the organisation to political theories upon which not even its own adult members are agreed.'[12]

The postwar abandonment of agreement to the Charter as a condition of membership did not fundamentally alter the political content of the Folk's educational activity. This was codified after the war in an educational program, the *Woodcraft Way*, written by Rawson. Building on the programme developed by Leslie Paul, this was in essence a variant of utopian socialism in which the permanent co-operative communes of Robert Owen were replaced by the short term co-operative community of the Woodcraft camp. Rawson expressed the views of many Folk members when stating that 'we must use camping as the reproduction of socialist communities in which our children learn by experience and practice a better and truer way of living'.[13] This involved taking of children out of urban society into ideal communities where they could experience co-operative living rather than the competition for jobs and services which dominated workers' lives in the city.

'Test work' carried out at group nights complemented these co-operative camps not only by providing children (and new leaders) with skills useful for camping, but also by drawing conclusions out of the camping experience about citizenship in the world at large. On completion of each test a child was awarded a badge which they could wear on their green Woodcraft shirt—thus it became known as 'badge work'. The *Woodcraft Way* addressed itself directly to the child and they were intended to use it as a manual of practical tests through which they could move at their own individual pace. Completing the tests was not seen as a competitive activity as many of the tests could only be carried out as part of a larger group or in the context of the co-operative camp. The badge was seen as a symbol of individual achievement rather than as a source of comparison with others, so only one could be sewn on the shirt at any one time. This was in effect the Folk's national curriculum, starting with camping and outdoor skills (crafts of the woods) and culminating in awareness as a 'Citizen' and 'World Citizen', and aiming to produce young people with the 'physical, mental and social fitness for world service'.[14]

Ceremonies were the third essential ingredient of Rawson's approach, and served to remind both adults and children of how they were working together for 'a great cause and great idea'. He explained:

> Much preferred to the parade and orders way of doing things, it is the
> Folk tradition to mark some of our actions in the group meeting and at
> camp, by special Ceremonies…it is in our ceremonies that we have
> another opportunity of expressing our ideas and the innermost truths of
> our Woodcraft Life.[15]

Ceremony and ritual in fact constituted the glue that enabled these islands
of socialist cooperation to function with a degree of democracy and efficiency that could so easily be undermined by the competitive attitudes
children (and adults) brought with them. It also helped render the partici-
pants more conscious of the difference between that community and the
mainstream of society—indeed it celebrated that difference.

This was the contradiction at the heart of the Folk's educational policy—
that its ability to create short term socialist communities in which children
'learnt by doing' was only possible through ceremonies and rituals which, in
drawing a line against the influences of everyday life, also served to emphasise their isolation and separateness from everyday life. This is why any
attempts to modify or update those ceremonies and traditions always caused
tension between 'modernisers' and 'traditionalists'.

The use of Folk names illustrates the point well. One member explained
how:

> The child's 'civilised' name was written on a piece of birch bark and
> thrown on the Council Fire after which he was given a chosen name…The
> ceremony was designed to impress the child with the idea that he was no
> longer a slave of 'Mannon' (sic) or 'the great God grind' but a rebel and
> one pledged to work for peace and friendship.[16]

The Folk name would be something of the woods—Badger or Little Otter.
According to Davis there were two apparently different justifications for the
use of Folk names. One was that it heightened camp democracy by avoiding children having to address adults as Sir or Miss at a time when first names
were not used in the mainstream. The other was that it 'emphasised the break
from everyday life and helped us assume another identity'.[17] Both were true.
As the modernisers sought to jettison the use of Folk names when first
names became more acceptable, the traditionalists attempted to defend what
they saw as an element of the Folk's separate identity—an identity that was
central to its educational role.

The modernisers too were caught in a contradiction when encountering
the youth culture that emerged in the 1950s. As Ken Jones points out, from

the Albermarle perspective there was an emerging generational conflict over culture, morality and values: 'Central to this conflict was that young workers had more money, and were targeted as consumers by a growing commercial popular culture, which reached out to those still at school.'[18] Many British educationalists believed that children had:

> rejected Britain for America, tradition for novelty, established values based on careful adult evaluation of children's needs for the instant gratification of children's wants. The sense of a cultural decline, in which childhood was implicated, and the focus on youth culture as a battleground of opposing forces, were commonplaces of the period.[19]

Educational practice thus set itself against the new culture and the school was defined as the custodian of traditional values.

The desire to resist what was seen as a decline in culture and values was also evident amongst the modernisers in the Folk. In 1965 a conference motion from Muswell Hill District stated:

> The child of today is confronted with a society in which there are many negative and destructive influences, such as the presentation of false values in films, television and pop music. Commercialism in culture requires a passive and uncritical teen age public and the Folk must become one of the major challenges to this trend.

Of course, the Folk did not see itself as championing the 'traditional values' that the school system was trying to shore up. It had its own tradition and culture that was contrary to that dominant in society. Basing itself on those values, and with updated 'songs of its own making' and Creeds in a language 'accessible to the children of the 1960s', it sought to challenge the destructive commercialised youth culture.[20] However within a few years both the traditional values of the establishment and the commercialism of the consumer society were to be challenged in a way the Folk did not then anticipate and which went way beyond the Folk's own critique—and this challenge came from young people themselves.

The youth radicalisation of the late 1960s was more than a continuation of the generation gap that emerged towards the end of the 1950s. By the late 1960s young people were not simply insisting that they were adults and finding themselves in conflict with teachers and parents who insisted that they were not. They celebrated their youth as something superior to adulthood, not 'as a preparatory stage of adulthood but, in some sense, as the final stage of human development.'[21] Anti-authoritarianism was one of the hall marks of this radicalisation, authority being identified as the previous generation's exercise of power within the family and society. According to Hobsbawm 'personal liberation and social liberation thus went hand in hand; the most obvious ways of shattering the bonds of state, parental and neighbours' power, law and convention, being sex and drugs.'[22] Rock and Roll was the third essential of cultural rebellion—this international form of communication became the crucial idiom through which the other two were reinforced.

This cultural identification was however taken to another level by the political internationalism of the late 1960s student movements, the leaders of which eagerly established contacts with members of their own generation across borders. Nor was this international youth radicalisation purely a middle-class phenomenon:

> This was patently true of the world-wide student movements, but where these sparked off mass labour uprisings, as in France and Italy in 1968-9, the initiative there also came from young workers.[23]

As the political radicalisation gained momentum it interacted with the cultural rebellion, combining 'an anti-consumerist stress on spiritual enjoyment, on love, Flower Power and individual self-fulfilment with older kinds of political visions—of social revolution, class war, strikes and barricades'.[24] Young people were not simply embracing a new youth culture, but increasingly utilising it not merely to construct their own critique of the traditional values now being undermined by social and cultural change, but also of the new commercial culture and consumer society itself—the same culture which the Folk had denounced in the 1965 resolution referred to above as requiring 'a passive and uncritical teenage public'. According to Mazower, against the background of the Vietnam War 'the children of the consumer revolution were now turning against it and coming back to politics and protest.'[25]

The Folk's response to the youth radicalisation was undoubtedly constrained by its response to 1950s youth culture. It was still struggling against what it saw as a purely commercial and consumerist youth culture. In 1970 it sought to combat 'the many undesirable features of substandard culture now being directed at and influencing young people, through mass media and commercial agencies' by improving the standard and content of its own cultural activities.[26] With hindsight Linda Osborn locates this response in the insular nature of the organisation whereby 'the older generation equated the new trend with materialism and exploitation of young people. To a certain extent they were right, but they also failed to recognise the power that they could have used to progress their ideas through the new mediums.'[27]

The wearing of folk costume was for many older members the most visual manifestation of the ability of the Folk to stand out against the commercialism which was potentially undermining not only the culture of society, but of the Folk too. On this issue some felt the best means of defence was attack. A 1967 conference resolution proposed that the description of 'costume' be changed to 'uniform'; that girls and women's skirts were to be grey and 'not subject to extreme fluctuations of fashion where length is concerned and, except in the case of Elfins, they shall not be shorter than two inches above the knee. The waist line will conform to the natural waist of the wearer.' Others baulked at such a direct confrontation with the youth culture, and the motion was altered beyond recognition in the confused debate.[28] In 1969 another resolution noted that leaders and helpers were often disregarding Folk Law when it came to the costume:

> This refusal to conform on the grounds of 'personal freedom', or for whatever egocentric reason, places an unfair burden on those leaders who insist upon conformity on the part of their own group members and sets a poor example of co-operative discipline.

Clearly many adult leaders were buckling under the pressure of the youth culture.[29]

It was easier for the Folk to respond to the political side of the radicalisation. This was primarily because responding to the internationalism that ran like a thread through the youth radicalisation, it was able to overcome its defensiveness and give space to young people to express that stance. The Folk's participation in international youth organisations and exchanges had begun before the war and was intensified after it. By the 1960s and 1970s, the national camps hosting foreign delegations held every four years were the high point of the Folk's calendar. In many respects this activity was in line with, and grew out of, the Folk's utopian socialist perspective. By 'spanning the world with friendship', by inviting children from other lands to your camps and visiting theirs, children could be educated in the ways of peace and international understanding. This was the core of the Folk's internationalism. However much more important than any ideological stance was the difference it made to the Folk's practice. It took the Folk out into the world and brought the concerns of the world into the Folk. The Folk's 'brave stand against the Cold War' was less to do with a clear class conscious perspective on the burning issues of the day than with a stubborn and principled refusal to abandon its utopian socialist commitment to educating children in international understanding through international exchanges. The cold war—and its potential for hot war—made it even more imperative to include children from behind the 'iron curtain' in those exchanges. In the early 1960s Folk members would leave conference early to join the last leg of the Aldermaston marches for nuclear disarmament because they saw themselves as part of an international movement against weapons that threatened the whole of humanity.[30]

The Folk responded within this framework to the US bombing of North Vietnam. The 1967 conference received a telegram from an anti-war march:

> Greetings ADC From March. We Ask You To Act To End Bombings And War In Vietnam. Woodcraft Peace Marchers.

The telegram was intended to increase support for the resolution submitted to conference by Muswell Hill District Association. It was carried unanimously, and this was due to the careful wording. Whilst clearly political in so far as it made a call on a Labour Government then complicit in the bombings to disassociate itself from them, it legitimised that stance on the grounds of enabling negotiations (in line with a UN appeal) and the consequences of the war for children. Many of the adult leaders who felt uncomfortable about a children's organisation taking a stand on political issues would have felt that it was legitimate to do so when relevant to the needs of children, regardless of where they lived. Furthermore the resolution refrained from taking clear sides in the conflict—it called for an end to the bombings to enable peace through negotiations rather than demanding the withdrawal of American troops.[31]

However it also gave those young people in the Folk who were increasingly drawn to the campaign for American withdrawal of troops an avenue for campaigning and discussion through collecting for Medical Aid for Vietnam. It was, to use the jargon, an 'enabling' resolution. It enabled increasingly radicalised young people to find an avenue to express their developing political views through the Folk. Had the Folk not responded to this radicalisation—on the issue of Vietnam above all—all its attempts to challenge the perceived materialism of youth culture would have been in vain. It was the internationalism of the Folk which enabled it to move outwards and retain in its ranks a layer of the 1968 generation.

Thus for Andy Piercy, who was a teenage member in the early 1960s, the clash of cultures and generations was overcome by the ability of the Folk to respond to the political concerns, particularly through international work, of their generation. Looking back he believes that:

> the Folk was unusual in the sense that some of the things that young people were concerned about…were also concerns of the leaders they were relating to. They shared that common vision. So my recollections are less of the Folk as folk music and more as folk politics as well, because there were a lot of issues relating to the Iron Curtain around in the sense that we were being criticised over who we were working with at an international level.

For Piercy the international links of the Folk provided a perfect forum for expressing his internationalist perspective.[32]

However others must surely have chosen to find new homes—either for cultural and 'lifestyle' experimentation or for political action, or both. Thus whilst the Folk had some success in establishing groups for the fourteen to seventeen age range, the results were not as good as might have been hoped. In 1968 the number of Venturer groups was twenty-eight, but this contrasted with 141 Elfin groups and 131 Pioneer groups.[33] In an organisation that is progressive in the sense that children start in the lowest age group and gradually progress up, some falling away is to be expected as they advance to each subsequent age range. This is particularly acute as teenagers begin to leave school and home, and find sexual partners. However, these figures show a seventy-nine per cent drop out rate during the transition from Pioneers to Venturers. In many districts Venturer groups simply did not exist.

One factor responsible for this lack of success was undoubtedly a continued reluctance on the part of many adults to establish these groups for fear of losing their trainee leaders. However even where Venturer groups were established there was a lack of clarity about the sort of programme they should be pursuing. When Basil Rawson had first initiated experimental Venturer groups it was assumed that the badge work of the *Woodcraft Way*—particularly the final badges on Citizenship and World Citizenship—would still form their core curriculum. At the same time it was assumed that this age group, though still having adult leaders, would take on far more responsibility for planning their own programme. The result was different groups adopting widely different practices, leading the general secretary to comment: 'I fear that now, except where we have exceptional leaders, our Venturer group could be nothing more than an open club.'[34]

Some improvement in numbers occurred when in 1971 constitutional changes brought the Venturer age down (thirteen to fifteen inclusive) and created a new category of Senior Venturers (sixteen and seventeen). By 1973 the number of Venturer groups was up to 38, and the first national camp for the Venturer age range attracted over 200 people. However there were only three Senior Venturer groups, and when little change had occurred by 1976 conference again lamented 'the loss of valuable members from the Folk of this age group'.[35]

Radical parents and the Folk

To appreciate the radical political content of the re-orientation of the Folk in the late 1970s and 1980s it is necessary to take into account the changed context in which it took place. The recession of 1975 saw the youth labour market collapse in Britain, and the gap between school and work left young people occupying a space that had the disciplining effects of neither. Policy makers saw signs of what they perceived as a fragmenting social order and, whilst this required responses that were beyond the capacity of schools, right-wing educationalists blamed progressive education in schools for adding to the problem. In 1975 William Tyndale Junior School became the focus of a press campaign because teachers there had 'implemented a radical version of a progressive curriculum, centring on free choice and the celebration of unauthorised cultures'.[36] Schools were failing, according to what was then being referred to as the 'new right', not because they were dealing with intractable problems of social inequality but because of the ideologies of progressive educators and the political commitments of a section of the teaching force. The youth service was increasingly looked to by government to 'target "areas of high social need" and the most troublesome young people with them.'[37]

It is in this context that attempts in 1975 and 1976 to smear the Folk should be understood. Such red-baiting was not new. In 1963 the *Sunday Telegraph* had alleged that the Folk was being infiltrated by members of the Communist Party.[38] By focusing on the political stance and activities of some of its members it was possible to imply that the Folk had a hidden party political agenda whilst avoiding discussing the practical educational activity which it actually carried out with children and young people. The Folk's youth exchanges across the iron curtain and the inclusion of songs from these countries in its songbook provided the 'evidence' for other charges of political indoctrination. What was new about the 1975 campaign was that it was prompted by a circular sent out by Conservative Central Office which asked for information from constituency parties on the Folk's applications to Labour controlled councils for youth service funding. The Folk had aligned itself with the Youth Service since the Albermarle report and was actively seeking local authority and government funding. As a consequence it came under fire from those who wished to blame educational failure on politically motivated progressivism. The *News of the World* picked up on the story, and such was the press coverage that in 1976 Margaret White appeared on *Nationwide*, a primetime current affairs and magazine television programme, to present the Folk's case.[39]

In the short term the Folk had to clarify its educational values and practice if its status in the Youth Service and its funding was to be maintained. In the longer term something more was at stake. These were just the opening skirmishes of a prolonged campaign by the Thatcherite right to recast the debate on education. This was not simply a matter of cutting back state expenditure (and with it educational opportunities) in line with the ending of the 'golden age' of post war capitalism. Where the right had been increasingly defeated by the social-democratic platform of 'equality of opportunity' which had dominated the post-war boom years, it was now recasting that debate by advancing on the terrain of educational content. However that terrain was already occupied. In the schools and local authorities the ranks of the progressive educationalists were being reinforced by those educated in the youth and student radicalisation of the 1960s and 1970s and from the new social movements, and they were adding their own gender, race and sexuality issues to that of class as items on the educational agenda. In the Youth Service young workers were subverting the pressures to target provision by expanding it for black youth and developing 'work with girls'. Over time greater centralisation of what could and could not be done in schools and the Youth Service closed down much of the space for experimentation, but this was a protracted process only finally completed in 1988 with the Education Reform Act, and even then not without conceding the inclusion of many of these issues in the national curriculum.[40]

The new terms of debate were clear even before the election of the Thatcher government in 1979. The Folk, having positioned itself as part of the Youth Service from 1960 onwards, could now either withdraw from that involvement or try and position itself within the new terms of debate. There was no disagreement within the Folk that it should take the latter course. What however was less clear was exactly how it should position itself in the debate. Up until now the utopian socialist framework of the Folk's educational policy had been taken for granted, absorbed as it were by osmosis as each new generation grew up in the Folk and became the next layer of leaders. The camping community, the sense of a common and separate identity, the continuity of the *Woodcraft Way*, its ceremony and tradition—these were the clear certainties that so encapsulated an educational practice that the educational practitioner need not even be consciously aware of the theory underlying it.

Now however, in response to the post-1975 climate, a new theoretical framework was beginning to emerge and gain influence in the Folk. This theorisation was developed by members of the Communist Party and other radicals who were influenced by the ideas of Eurocommunism and by the journal *Marxism Today*. Utilising Gramsci's ideas on how the capitalist class maintained its rule not simply through the coercive power of the state's repressive apparatus but also through its ideological hegemony, Eurocommunists advocated the creation of alternative ideological, political, cultural and moral alliances that could enable the working class to challenge capitalist hegemony. In the field of education in the late 1970s and 1980s this approach meant forging a broad alliance around educational values and an educational practice that could meet the ideological challenge increasingly posed by the new right. The educational values were provided by, and could draw on the social strength of, the new social movements that had emerged as a result of 1968. The educational practice was a re-modelling of the Folk's 'learn by doing'—instead of emphasising the separateness of the socialist camping community as a means of educating children for socially aware adulthood, it stressed meeting the educational needs of children and youth that arose from their actual lives within capitalist society by using the co-operative camping community to explore those issues.[41]

The first significant step in a process of reorientation was taken in 1979 when conference discussed a series of changes to the constitution. Perhaps the most important in terms of Rawson's commitment to gradualist socialist change through education was the section on 'Education for Social Change' which stated:

> We seek to develop in our members a critical awareness of the world in which they grow up. We urge them to seek and accept their responsibilities as citizens and to participate in the democratic process in order to bring about the changes that they feel are necessary, to create a caring society.'[42]

This was both a defensive formula, since the Folk could not be accused of indoctrination where their members were being encouraged to decide for themselves the changes that needed making in society, and at the same time a challenge to the educational mainstream to encourage, and have confidence in, young people making such choices for themselves.

Also included in the new constitution were sections on the rights of the child, equality between men and women and the environment. Again these educational values were a challenge to those on the right, but the Folk could justify their inclusion not because they contributed towards developing a socialist consciousness amongst children that they could draw on in their later adult lives, but because they were issues that directly confronted young people in their pre-adult lives.

At this stage the broad thrust of this and other constitutional changes were not in dispute. Longstanding members rightly felt that the Folk had always sought to educate for social change, and had always been aware of the rights of the child.[43] Indeed the impetus for change in fact came from longstanding members.[44] Yet the implications of this re-orientation for the Folk's established practice—its camping traditions, educational program and ceremonies—were still to be clarified. Over the next two years these questions about practical issues led to unanticipated explosions of tension within the Folk's established leadership. Furthermore a large scale influx of new adult members during early 1980s fully revealed the underlying causes of these tensions.

The main channel for this influx of new members was CND and the anti Cruise Missile mobilisations of the early 1980s. In 1981 a new clause was added to the Folk constitution on 'A World at Peace'. Leaflets distributed at demonstrations carried messages such as 'We don't inherit the world from our ancestors; we borrow it from our children.'[45] Angela Downing, who became a group leader in Manchester in 1980, describes the type of people the Folk began to attract at this time thus:

> I would say a lot of the new leaders had been student activists in the International Socialists, or in more libertarian groups such as whole food co-ops, homelessness pressure groups…Some were in religious groups …All were peace activists in Manchester. At work they were involved in equal opportunities, and probably all in trade unions but found that rather dull. Some were involved in gay politics too.[46]

This influx enabled a rapid increase in the number of groups which continued throughout the 1980s—the fact that the greatest gains were in Elfin groups confirms oral testimony that these new recruits were mainly parents of young children.

With such a rapid influx of people with no tradition of activity in the Folk, and their own ideas on what they wanted from the Folk, it was inevitable that educational practices on the ground would become more diversified and conflict would arise. According to Downing 'we used themes, not the badge work programme…to reach issues and that would include co-operative games, dance, song, stories, dramas, crafts, food and the outdoors'.[47]

As a consequence two different Woodcrafts were emerging; one which was rooted in tradition, including the educational programmes based on 'badge work', and the other experimenting with broad themes and incorporating materials from the peace, anti-racist and women's movements. At group and often district level it was possible for these different approaches to co-exist within the Folk because each approach was implemented in its own separate space. Again Downing recalls:

There was no immediate clash of cultures as we were all new together and stayed apart from the older groups. When we met them we were amazed and often shocked. So were they at us. But there were positives and some individuals were inspiring, heroic, welcoming, shared their skills and knowledge and were very supportive. So it's not a straightforward situation. Overall the traditional groups in this area were weak…and as new groups opened there was mutual tolerance but not much sharing.[48]

However mutual tolerance became more difficult when the new members challenged the long-established ceremonies and traditions of the Folk.

Mary Davis argues that the Folk was late, compared with 'other labour movement organisations', in coming to grips with issues like racism and sexism. She finds it surprising that on the issue of sexism in particular the Folk 'appeared not to have noticed what had been going on elsewhere', given that it had always had women leaders and a formal commitment to sex equality. One explanation for this is that the radicalised youth who began to take these issues up in other organisations in the 1970s only turned to the Folk in larger numbers in the 1980s on becoming parents. This greatly amplified the voices of those younger members who had already begun to raise these issues during the 1970s. However an equally important reason is the specific manner in which the Folk's previous commitment to sex and race equality intertwined with its utopian socialist theorisation of its practical camping activity.

In 1976 the Folk magazine *New Day* had debated the issue of why there were so few women on Council. Whilst those younger members influenced by the women's movement suggested changes in how the Folk organised conferences and meetings to make them more accessible for women with young children, a survey of members in two districts suggested that while at group and camp level women members felt themselves to be equals:

Time and family commitments prevent most women doing more at District and national level. This does not mean there is no equal opportunity within the Folk; the opportunities are there but the vast majority of women cannot accept them.[49]

Of course it was this gap between formal and actual equality, and the unequal position of women within the family underlying this, that was being challenged by the women's movement in broader society. Even though Woodcraft Folk members were becoming aware of those debates this did not lead to an automatic recognition of the gap between formal and actual equality in the Folk itself.

This is more explicable if we bear in mind the sense of equality and comradeship that was engendered in the Folk's camps. Whilst the Woodcraft camp was not in practice the socialist utopia that it was theorised to be, it felt very unlike everyday life not just because of the ceremony and ritual that acted to reinforce that difference, but because in one crucial respect it was different. At camp there was no separation between the spheres of work and home or of work and childcare. Even though the division of labour amongst adults often reflected a gendering carried over from the outside world (women usually being responsible for food ordering and men for emptying toilets), all adults were collectively responsible for both child care, cooking and other tasks. In order to ensure the care and equal involvement of the many children not accompanied by their parents or carers, adults saw themselves as collectively caring for all the children and not just their own children. So although the Folk was often described as a 'family organisation' the family simply did not function in the same way on camp as at home.

When, with all the self-confidence (perhaps bordering on arrogance) of that generation, the influx of the 1980s began raising social issues as though no-one had struggled with them before, this could not but provoke a reaction from longstanding women members. Looking back on these discussions Doug Bourn, who succeeded Margaret White as general secretary in 1983, argues that prior to the emergence of the women's liberation movement:

> For the majority of women in the Folk their liberation and their confidence grew from the Folk, it didn't come from society outside. So everything they gained in their own personal development—such as women who then went on to become teachers, young working class women who went into the caring professions as opposed to domestic work or whatever—they got that from the Folk....So when younger people start to say that the Folk was not providing space for women to

articulate their needs they say: 'I'm sorry that's not true, I've got every-thing I wanted from the Folk'.[50]

With this in mind it is easier to understand why the immediate response of many longstanding members was denial. In 1982, when a debate was opened in the Folk magazine, *Focus*, on the gendered wording of ceremonies and songs, Wad Klos argued:

> I am aware of the sexist attitudes which prevail throughout society and I would unequivocally urge all our members to speak out against these atti-tudes...What I cannot accept however is that these attitudes prevail in our organisation.

Ironically in the same issue as this letter was published another corre-spondent commented that 'equality can only go so far. Biologically we are different, a fact which is often forgotten by ardent feminists.'[51] Klos would certainly have been aware that many men within the Folk held the view that equality should stop somewhere short of complete equality. The only explanation of his insistence that these views did not prevail in the Folk is that, more important than individual attitudes, at camp members expe-rienced a sense of equality and co-operation that went well beyond that of everyday life.

The fact that it was the gendered wording of ceremonies and songs that was being challenged added greatly to the tensions surrounding this debate. For many members these were part of a Folk tradition which both enabled the Woodcraft camp to run smoothly and which helped to defend the prin-ciples for a better world which the Woodcraft camp embodied. As Barbara Colbert put it in a letter to *Focus*:

> One of the real values of tradition is that it can dispense with the need for a rule...New members, including adults, will often readily accept cus-tom, rather than a long list of dos and don'ts.

Whilst accepting that customs could be changed by common consent, she stressed '...the influence exerted by custom and habit in maintaining a prin-ciple. If we stop believing in a principle then our lack of faith will ensure that it dies out. If we retain our belief then tradition will help support it.'[52] From this perspective the weakening of ceremony and tradition was a blow to the essence of the Folk's educational role—indeed, as with the decreas-ing use of the *Woodcraft Way*, it was perceived as leading to practice devoid

of any coherent educational content. For those wishing to place a new interpretation on 'Education for social change' these ceremonies and traditions
simply did not play the same vital role—indeed they were seen as potentially
counter-productive by appearing to contradict the educational values essential to engaging with the everyday lives of children and young people.[53]

In one age group in particular the difficulties of maintaining the role of
test work, ceremony and tradition was more sharply posed—amongst
youth. As Colbert observed 'it seems that the older children get the less priority they put on badges.'[54] Tensions over how to respond to the challenges
to ceremony and tradition made by young people themselves had been present since the 1960s and surfaced again with the post-1975 youth culture of
unemployment and disillusionment, punk. For those who were by the early
1980s concerned with the apparent willingness of both established and new
leaders to abandon ceremony and tradition, nowhere was this more clearly
manifested than in the relaxation of those traditions amongst the Venturer
age group.

By 1984 the new orientation was dominant within the leadership of the
Folk. Council member Tony Winsloe, perhaps its leading theoretician,
expressed it this way in *Focus*:

> We are now recognised as part of the mainstream of the Youth Service
> and ideas that we have held dear for years are now common to a number
> of youth organisations, in varying degrees. We stand with them on social
> education, racialism, peace and many other ideas.

Pointing to the section of the Folk constitution that prevented it being
involved in the activities and policy making of political parties he argued that,
whilst this was necessary to maintain the Folk's status in the Youth Service
and as a charity, this was not the only reason:

> I believe it to be educationally vital. For this reason we limit our policy
> aims to ideas which are so universal in their concepts that the principle
> can be explained to our youngest members in terms of right and
> wrong....As children grow they will certainly want to find out the rea-
> soning behind more complex ideas....but they must be allowed to set their
> own pace. To impose predetermined adult political concepts on children
> runs contrary to genuine educational discovery.[55]

The dominance of this new approach was made possible by the influx of
new members, but this influx also contained its own contradictions. In 1985

Peggy Aprahamian complained about the 'liberal revolutionaries' who appeared to want to reshape the Woodcraft Folk in their own image:

> Strong minded and middle class they are likely to try and do so. They are not prepared to accept the movement as it is and to propose changes to 'what is' but rather they are hyper-critical, to the point where one wonders why they have joined. They are against the shirt, against defined forms of leadership and very sentimental about their *own* children.[56]

In 1987 the new national secretary, Doug Bourn, also alerted members to the dangers of middle-class members being sentimental about their own children:

> The Woodcraft Folk can too easily become a haven for an 'alternative culture'—a retreat—leading to exclusiveness and being too closely knit. The social needs of the community somehow become lost. Folk groups become middle class elitist havens, often even worse white havens in black communities.

This is why he now placed so much stress on development work then being pioneered in Scotland which was attempting to establish groups in new working-class communities. From this perspective the exclusiveness of the traditional 'Folk Culture' was just as much a barrier to such development as inward looking middle-class exclusiveness.[57]

Yet being aware of the social needs of the community—and not just their own children—had been the great strength of the working-class leaders of the Folk. This is why they had progressed from being members of the Folk as children to being leaders, and why they had remained leaders after their own children had grown up. This is why they had sought to establish groups not simply within their own immediate community, but where they felt there was the most need for the Folk's educational role. Just as women had felt empowered by the Folk, so working-class youth had discovered their capacity for leadership at the Woodcraft camp. For many such leaders the new orientation represented an abandonment of that commitment to a broader community and the working-class community in particular and this resulted in some members withdrawing from the Folk:

> There seems to be an attitude within the Folk that the old outdoor skills and traditions are too escapist to be of any use. Escapism may not deal directly with many of today's social problems, but it does provide a wel-

come break and that alone is a profitable tool of social change…..from being an essentially working class outdoor organisation the Folk has turned into a dumping ground for middle class trendies with a social conscience to off load their offspring.[58]

A changed organisation

I have not attempted to make a thorough evaluation of the successes and failures of this repositioning of the Folk. Incontestably the rapid and sustained growth of the 1980s was reversed in the 1990s. Only a thorough researching of the 1990s history of the Folk could throw light on all the reasons for this. However in one respect the Folk is a changed organisation—the balance of the age groups within the Folk, despite the overall decline in the number of groups, has shifted towards a greater involvement of youth groups. In 1989, recognising that they needed their own identity and programme of activities, the Folk established a national District Fellowship (DF) structure for sixteen to twenty year olds. Furthermore a national conference of these younger members could elect four members of council with full voting rights. Diane Fairfax, former council member and strong supporter of this change at the time believed that it was important 'because we were purporting to be a children and young people's organization but were still controlling their involvement. This was about empowering the DFs to have greater influence in the way the movement was run.'[59]

This raises another issue. Given that the mainstream of education, including the national curriculum, has apparently accommodated so many of the issues that the 1968 generation demanded, is there any radical content left to the Folk that would warrant its being seen as still offering a 'progressive alternative'? The current general secretary, Andy Piercy, certainly thinks so:

It is great that these issues have become mainstream. But…people may have policies, but they may have them because they have to have them, rather than making them effective…For example when so many people walked out of school before we went to war and invaded Iraq, our Pioneers were discussing how unfair it was for somebody to be disciplined when the teacher was encouraging them to discuss the issues. And they did discuss the issues and when they did something about it some got suspended. You encourage them to think for themselves and when you don't like what they thought, then you have a problem.[60]

Rachel Schon, now fifteen, was a member of the Folk from five years old. She was a member of the Folk's delegation to the Earth Summit in Johannesburg, 2002, which presented the 2001 Woodcraft Camp declaration on sustainability. Her comments on empowerment seem pertinent:

> Woodcraft Folk is very radical in...it listens to its membership. I don't think the Woodcraft Folk as an organisation politicises its membership. I think it is receptive to what the membership think and it tries to support that...They try to make their members people who don't feel that they can't do anything, who can investigate things and be self-sufficient.[61]

That last sentence is in total continuity with Basil Rawson.

Notes

1. Eric Hobsbawm, *Age of Extremes. The short twentieth century* (London, 1994), p.324.
2. Basil Rawson, 'Discussion paper prepared for the 1961 Conference', Woodcraft Folk (WF) archives held at the LSE. Many documents from these archives can be found on the Woodcraft Folk website <http://www.woodcraft.org.uk>. Copiesof *Woodcraft Focus* and *New Day* will also be found in the WF archives. All interviews cited were conducted by the author during 2003.
3. I have used The Folk as short hand for the Woodcraft Folk because that is the shorthand that the organisation itself uses. They also had many names for different bodies and events which are less comprehendible to us today, and these were modernised and modified over the years that this article covers. To make things easier for the reader I have used the following terms in this article: *conference* for the Annual Delegate Conference (ADC) now called National Gathering; *council* for the elected national leadership body called variously National Folk Council, National Council and General Council; *group* for the weekly sessions organised by age groups that children and youth join, at one time called fellowships and lodges; and *district* for the structure that draws together the adults running the different groups in a geographical locality, at one time called Things.
4. Referring to the early years of the Folk, Paul wrote: 'How genuine, however, was our belief that one had to "learn by doing, teach by being".' Leslie Paul, *The Early Days of the Woodcraft Folk* (London, 1980), p.10.
5. Mary Davis, *Fashioning a New World* (Loughborough, 2000).
6. Davis, *New World*, pp.111-15
7. Report of the departmental committee on The Youth Service in England and Wales, also known as the Albermarle Report, cited in Ken Jones, *Education in Britain: 1944 to the present* (Cambridge, 2003), pp.42-3.
8. Davis, *New World*, p.109.
9. WF Archives, file on 1961 ADC.

10. Interview with Margaret White.
11. WF Archives, Minutes of the 1963 ADC.
12. Cited by Davis, *New World*, p.64.
13. Cited by Davis, *New World*, p.105; see also interview with Margaret White.
14. For the changing role of the *Woodcraft Way* see Barbara Colbert, 'History of the Woodcraft Way', May 1986, Education Committee documents (WF archives).
15. Basil Rawson, *The Woodcraft Way* (London, 1961 edn), p.296.
16. Henry Fair reminiscing in 'Yesterday and Today', *Woodcraft Focus*, February 1982. Clearly the intended reference here is Mammon, the god of riches.
17. Davis, *New World*, p.104.
18. Jones, *Education*, p.42
19. Jones, *Education*, p.43.
20. WF archives, ADC minutes 1965.
21. Hobsbawm, *Age of Extremes*, p.325.
22. Hobsbawm, *Age of Extremes*, p.333.
23. Hobsbawm, *Age of Extremes*, p.324.
24. Mark Mazower, *Dark Continent: Europe's twentieth century* (London, 1998), p.322.
25. Mazower, *Dark Continent*, p.323
26. WF archives, ADC Minutes 1970.
27. Interview with Linda Osborn.
28. WF archives, 1967 ADC
29. WF archive, 1969 ADC. The 1969 revised and amended constitution states that men and boys should wear dark trousers and shorts for ceremonial occasions and appropriate times at camp. Women and girls should wear a grey, brown, navy blue or green skirt. At camp or hikes shorts or dark slacks to be permitted but skirts for all ceremonial occasions.
30. Interestingly the Folk avoided taking any clear cut position on either to the Cuban missile crisis of 1962 or the Soviet-led invasion of Czechoslovakia in 1968.
31. WF archives, ADC minutes, 1967.
32. Interview with Andy Piercy.
33. These figures are based on a handwritten 'announcement' to the 1968 ADC in the WF archives. Figures for 1973 onwards are taken from the annual report of the corresponding year. My thanks to Paul Bemrose for pointing out some of the difficulties in interpreting these figures.
34. WF archives, national council reports, report by Margaret White, 25 October 1969.
35. WF archives, conference minutes, 1971, 1973 and 1976.
36. Jones, *Education*, p.96.
37. B. Davies, *From Thatcherism to New Labour: A history of the Youth Service In England Volume 2, 1979-1999* (Leicester, 1999), pp.8-9.
38. Davis, *New World*, p.65.
39. Davis, *New World*, pp.109-10.
40. Whilst not doing justice to them, the sources which inspire this thumbnail sum-

mary of an extended process are Jones, *Education* and Davies, *From Thatcherism to New Labour*.

41. The influence of discussions on socialist strategy contained in *Marxism Today* is made explicit in an interview with Doug Bourn, 2003, and in an earlier draft volume by Bourn intended for publication in 1988 and now in the WF archives.
42. WF Archives, 1979 conference minutes.
43. Interview with Margaret White.
44. Interview with Diane Fairfax.
45. Interview with Doug Bourn.
46. Interview with Angela Downing.
47. Interview with Angela Downing.
48. Interview with Angela Downing.
49. Arnold Posner, 'Women in the leadership', *New Day*, August 1976; Linda Osborn and Josie Burnett, 'Women in the Folk 1 & 2', *New Day*, October 1976.
50. Interview with Doug Bourn.
51. *Woodcraft Focus*, May 1982.
52. Letter from Barbara Colbert, *Woodcraft Focus*, February 1982.
53. I have concentrated here on the issue of sexism and gender. For reasons of space I cannot explore the issue of race. However, here too the 'modernisers' saw the ceremonies and customs of the Folk as being essentially a barrier to racial inclusiveness.
54. Barbara Colbert, 'History of the Woodcraft Way', May 1986 (WF Archives, Education Committee documents).
55. Tony Winsloe, 'Politics and the full stop', *Woodcraft Focus*, spring 1984.
56. WF Archives, Education Committee papers, Peggy Aprahamian, 'Report on leader training course', 19-24 August 1985, dated 3 September 1985.
57. WF Archives Doug Bourn, national secretary, address to WF annual delegate conference, 4 April 1987.
58. WF archives, A.B. Hall, letter of resignation from WF and WF council, 23 January 1986.
59. Interview with Diane Fairfax.
60. Interview with Andy Piercy.
61. Interview with Rachel Schon.

'The Hippies Now Wear Black'

Crass and the anarcho-punk movement, 1977–84

Richard Cross

Few social historians of Britain in the late 1970s would dismiss the influence that the emergent punk rock movement exerted in the fields of music, fashion and design, and art and aesthetics. Most would accept too that the repercussions and reverberations of punk's challenge to the suffocating norms against which it rebelled so vehemently continue to be felt in the present tense.[1] Behind the tabloid preoccupation with the Sex Pistols, a maelstrom of bands, including such acts as The Damned, The Buzzcocks, Slaughter and the Dogs, X-Ray Spex and The Raincoats, together redefined the experience of popular music and its relationship to the cultural mainstream. Bursting into the headlines as the unwelcome gatecrasher of the Silver Jubilee celebrations, punk inspired the misfits and malcontents of a new generation to reject the constraints of an exhausted post-war settlement, and to rail against boredom, alienation, wage-slavery, and social conformity.

Yet, in retrospect, the purity of punk's 'total rejection' of 'straight society' (if not seen as comprised from the outset) appears fleeting. By the tail-end of 1977, the integrity of punk's critique seemed to be fast unraveling. What had declared itself to be an uncompromising cultural and musical assault on an ossified status quo, was becoming increasingly ensnared in the processes of 'incorporation' and 'commodification'. Punk bands which had earlier denounced the corporate big-time were signing lucrative deals with major record labels, keen to package and promote their rebellious messages. Specialist retailers, mimicking punk's innovate experiments with fashion and adornment, began to market new lines of standardised punk clothing. Punk rock's non-negotiable hostility to the marketplace and the mainstream appeared to be collapsing. It had, in the words of one cynical observer been 'bought up, cleaned up, souped up' to become 'just another cheap product for the consumer's head'.[2] Yet at the same time that punk appeared to be losing its way, a current emerged within the movement declaring itself committed to the prosecution of the punk ideal and determined to rediscover what it saw as punk's authentic and original intent.

The story of the birth of punk rock in Britain and the US is being rehearsed in ever-greater detail in the burgeoning historiography of this 'new wave' of music, fashion, art and culture—which, alongside individual biography, offers accounts of different subcultures within punk, and treatments of local scenes and time frames.[3] Yet, despite the proliferation of such studies in recent years, the political history of punk is painfully underdeveloped. The history of what can be claimed as the most intensely radical expression of punk's politics and aesthetic—anarcho-punk—remains almost entirely unrecorded. In the flood of publications addressing different aspects of the punk phenomenon that have appeared in the last few years, it is striking how often the experience of anarcho-punk is absent.[4] Although a few short treatments of Crass have been published,[5] most of the key debates currently animating both the academic and the popular literature on punk simply exclude anarcho-punk from their frame of reference.[6] This is an all the more glaring omission given the sophistication of anarcho-punk's own critique of punk practice, and the profound significance which Crass and other artists invested in the medium of punk.[7] In part, the exclusion of anarcho-punk from the majority of histories of the genre is a reflection of the reluctance of many authors to confront anarcho-punk's critique of 'conventional' punk's own practice. Yet, it is also the unintended consequence of anarcho-punk's own fiercely independent sensibilities, which often resulted in its effective separation from punk rock's own 'orthodox' mainstream.

Centred around the work of the band Crass, anarcho-punk asserted a belief in the politics and practice of punk 'as it was always supposed to have been'—autonomous, subversive and free from commercial corruption. Embracing the politics of anarchism, anti-militarism and pacifism, Crass worked to popularise the notion of a consciously revolutionary punk rock culture. It was an approach that inspired many thousands to immerse themselves in the highly distinctive 'do-it-yourself' (DIY) milieu of anarcho-punk and to commit their energies to what were recognised as the critical political struggles of the hour. The results of this 'reclamation' of the punk imperative were often remarkable, but as the years passed it became clear that the movement was struggling to realise what it hoped was its true potential. Because it thrived with little permanent structural form, anarcho-punk existed as an intriguing example of a movement defined by the contours of its subculture.

The emergence of anarcho-punk

In 1978, the release of the debut mini-album *The Feeding of the Five Thousand* by the band Crass announced the birth of a new current within the evolving British punk movement which came to be celebrated—and sometimes derided—as 'anarcho-punk'.[8] Musically, anarcho-punk certainly represented a further recalibration of the punk sound. After the Sex Pistols' *Never Mind the Bollocks*, or the self-titled first album by The Ramones, only a handful of records comprehensively reinvented the notion of what a punk rock album could sound like. In that, Crass's early releases could stand alongside artists as diverse as Joy Division and Discharge. When *The Feeding of the 5000* was released it sounded like no other punk record before it had—the signature military drum-beat; the skittery power-buzz of the two guitars; the relentless lyric-chewing vocal; the shift without pause from one song to another; the lack of rock pretensions. Even more notable than the musical content was its presentation—from the stunning, disturbing cover artwork, and the densely typed lyric sheet, to the uncompromising, compelling polemic with which the whole package bristled. It would be just these jarring juxtapositions between the content of the message and the medium of delivery that would give this new subculture so distinctive an edge, and infuse it with an infectious appeal that quickly attracted the interest of tens of thousands of young punks and displaced radicals.

The anthemic track 'Punk Is Dead' encapsulated the tension at the heart of what Crass were about, and what anarcho-punk would become—a band and a movement that at the same time both embraced and shunned, celebrated and denounced, punk:

> I see the velvet zippies in their bondage gear / The social elite with safety pins in their ear / I watch and understand that it don't mean a thing / The scorpions might attack, but the system stole the sting.[9]

As drummer Penny Rimbaud subsequently explained, this critique of punk was also intended as a rebuttal to what was perceived as the nihilistic declaration by Sex Pistols' front-man Johnny Rotten that there was to be 'no future'.[10] Even though the ever-resourceful Rotten has since rejected pessimistic readings of this lyric as shortsighted, Crass were, in contrast, claiming punk as a rallying cry to 'make history' rather than as the soundtrack for its end.[11]

Although a sizeable youth movement quickly burgeoned around them, Crass's position as the catalyst and engine for anarcho-punk was never seriously in question—however awkward Crass felt about their 'leading role'. Most of those involved with Crass were significantly older than the people who bought their records and came to their concerts. Unlike the majority of their contemporaries, Crass sought to highlight connections between the aspirations of 1960s counter-culture and the original impetus of 1970s punk. Importantly, Crass claimed punk as an extension and redefinition of elements brought forward from the culture of hippy. Several of the occupants of the Dial House commune from which Crass emerged had had long associations with hippy and other counter-cultural movements.[12] This notion of a rekindled hippy ethos sat problematically with punk's insistence on outright rejection of the political and musical forms of the past, but punk—drawing, as it had to do, on antecedents of all kinds—could not sustain the pretence that 1976 was some kind of 'year zero'. More problematic than hippy's pre-punk origins, was its content—and the difficulty of reconciling The Clash's declarations of 'hate and war' with Crass's insistence on 'love and peace'. Ultimately, such approaches could not be reconciled, even though both claimed to be legitimate representations of punk. Even so, Crass's was never an uncritical reading of hippy, but rather a reclamation of what were seen as common principles—a rejection of crushing social conventions; of miserable wage-labour; of war and militarism; and a celebration of freedom, both collective and individual. It was also, as many of the band's critics appeared slow to acknowledge, a vision of hippy which offered its own bi-polar view—castigating the self-satisfied hedonism of sixties counter-culture, whilst romanticising its more consciously political elements. The band's assertion of a counter-cultural continuity linking hippy and punk immediately aroused the suspicion of some within the punk movement concerned to protect punk from the contagion of the 'failures' of earlier generations. Disappointment with the decline and corrosion of hippy may help to explain the intensity of Crass's subsequent investment in punk. It had to work where hippy had failed. In their farewell written statement, Crass insist that the anarcho-punk brand of punk rock had eventually become 'almost synonymous with punk'.[13] They may have wished that this had been so, but in fact things were more complex. In reality, anarcho-punk was in perpetual contest with 'mainstream' punk, its take on the punk project opposed, ignored and challenged by those who saw their own readings as equally (or indeed more) authentic.

Anarcho-punk reclaimed the notion of punk autonomy—rejecting all approaches from the pop industry, establishing in their place the movement's own record labels and distribution networks; working directly and collaboratively, without agents or intermediaries, to set up tours, produce publications and record music. Remarkably, none of the bands whose reputation gave them a national, and indeed international, profile broke this self-imposed embargo to 'sell-out' to the majors. Crass themselves were approached by a would-be impresario, already responsible for a roster of mainstream acts, offering to 'market' the band's revolutionary message through the established channels. His offer of a large advance and a lucrative deal was summarily dismissed. In 1984, the band were amused to reject a tentative expression of interest in their work from thinly-disguised representatives of the Soviet Embassy in London—but not before Crass's own delegation had sunk the supply of vodka on offer from the agents of the Russian 'literary magazine' who had invited them for talks.[14] All aspects of the group's work, from its appearance on stage, the packaging of its records, to the band's relationship to its 'fans' were subject to a political critique which, it is claimed, tried to subvert usual rock'n'roll conventions, to reclaim what were seen as the essentials of 'punk'. Messages of anarchy, peace and love were now delivered in anguished howls, over distorted guitar riffs and thundering drum beats, by bands who sought to honour the principles of 'do-it-yourself punk' in every aspect of their work—records were stamped with the instruction to 'pay no more than' the breakeven price fixed by the band; concert tickets were sold for the barest minimum; all of the affectations and decadence of the rock-star lifestyle were shunned; and genuine efforts made to minimise the gap between performer and audience.

By 1984, the year in which Crass disbanded (a cut-off point set by the band in 1977), the anarcho-movement had reached the height of its powers, and was beginning to strain against its own political and sub-cultural limitations, and encroaching sense of fatigue.[15] Throughout the intervening years Crass remained the central focus and organising hub for anarcho-punk, at the heart of a network of bands, labels, artists and publications which rallied around the anarcho-punk banner, and which, taken together, loosely defined this movement within a movement.

A defining feature of anarcho-punk was the refusal to co-operate with the established music industry on all levels. To the consternation and incredulity of many music journalists Crass and other anarcho-bands declined to be interviewed and photographed for the pages of *Sounds*, the *NME* or *Melody Maker*. Instead anarcho-punk sought to stimulate its own outlets for its message, through the distinctive network of fanzines, and through handouts, mailings and publications under its own imprint, where control over content and presentation remained total, and unsullied by pop trivia around it. Crass's own position on the question was not absolute. When controversy propelled the band into the limelight, members of the group would appear on television and radio shows, to put an anarchist case, but the band's own minimum criteria for participation usually made such appearances difficult to agree. Despite the efforts of many officials in the pop industry to exclude them (a fate earlier endured by the Sex Pistols) Crass's records regularly sold sufficient quantities to break into the Top Thirty of the BBC's chart. There was no prospect of the BBC's producers agreeing to appearances by the band (they had only to cite the band's 'unbroadcastable' lyrics and the court actions for 'obscenity' that were a recurrent and unwelcome by-product of the band's published work), but Crass had their own impossible counter demand. Asked by *Tongue in Cheek* fanzine if there were any circumstances in which they would agree to appear on *Top of the Pops*, Crass replied: 'That we could talk uninterrupted on any subject of our choice for the length of time that the record that got us there took to play.'[16]

Such uncompromising statements of independence were, of course, criticised for being wilfully counter-productive, by those arguing that the most effective acts of subversion were undertaken from within the industry—who heralded the Pistols and other as the 'poison in the machine'—and not by those denouncing it from the outside. As the movement mushroomed, Crass could counter that their own practice was drawing the attention of tens of thousands of young people to anarchist ideas on an unprecedented scale, something that the movement's incorporation into the pop industry would immediately jeopardise. For Crass, the position remained self-evident:

We believed that you could no more be a socialist [band] and signed to CBS (The Clash) than you could be an anarchist and signed to EMI.[17]

Crass also powerfully asserted that if the practice of anarcho-punk was to mean anything, then it was self-evident that it had to demonstrate the validity of its precursor politics. Anarcho-punk performers everywhere insisted that it would trivialise and diminish their revolutionary message to align themselves with those complicit in reducing punk to product—by this time typified by the transformation of Adam and the Ants from a darkly sexualised art-punk ensemble into a sanitised pre-teen pop machine—and expose their DIY manifestos to ridicule.

And yet, inevitably, the integrity of anarcho-punk was sustained at no little cost. The movement's reliance on its own networks and outlets meant that to those engaged with it, the movement could appear vibrant and vital. But many outside of the immediate punk subculture were almost entirely unaware of its work. The movement's high principles made the negotiation

of alliances difficult, but the very completeness of anarcho-punk's own defiant subcultural independence made it difficult for the movement to
accurately assess its own political and cultural worth.

The politics of anarcho-punk

The politics espoused through the medium of anarcho-punk reflected a hec-
tic and eclectic mix of aspirations—which drew as much on moral as on
material considerations. There was no singular ideology in play, with—in
Crass's case—inspiration being drawn from Gandhian principles, radical philosophy, the aesthetics of the Beat and Bohemian poets, and the words of
Rimbaud and Baudelaire, as much as from the formal anarchist tradition.
Crass probably overstate the case when they claim that in the bands' early
days they 'probably would have thought' that Bakunin 'was a brand of
vodka',[18] but the profound suspicion of ideologues and fixed ideologies
remained. It afforded a politics largely free of debilitating baggage, but at
the same time the anchor points that it provided were few and far between.

Initially replete with expletives and rich in harsh invective, Crass's own writing and pronouncements developed into what were often sophisticated, lucid
and poetic writings. Alongside early songs such as 'Fight War, Not Wars' (the
only lyrics those of the title), came such detailed and intensely argued
polemics as 'Bumhooler', 'Rival Tribal Rebel Revel', and 'Bloody Revolutions',
and spoken word pieces such as 'Demoncrats', which concludes:

> Taken aside, they were pointed a way,
> For God, Queen and Country. Now in silence they lie.
>
> They ran before these masters, children of sorrow
> as slaves to that trilogy they had no future.
>
> They believed in democracy, freedom of speech,
> yet dead on the flesh piles I hear no breath,
> I hear no hope, no whisper of faith,
> from those that have died for some others' privilege.
>
> Out from your palaces, princes and queens,
> out from your churches, you clergy, you Christs,
> I'll neither live nor die for your dreams.
>
> I'll make no subscription to your paradise.[19]

Many other bands and performers within the anarcho-punk orbit chose a less poetic and literary timbre, grounding their work in the language and iconography of the radical campaigns and issues of the day. Crass's own reading of anarchism retained hippy's concern with the freedom of the individual from the intrusions of the state, but infused it with militant opposition to the 'war machine', and an excoriating critique of the alienated social relations of capitalism. In Crass's original lexicon, anarchism and pacifism were seen as synonymous and symbiotic. Around the calls for 'anarchy, peace and freedom', anarcho-punk's varied political impulses pushed the movement in diverse directions. Anti-militarism and, in particular, opposition to the nuclear arms race, remained definitional concerns throughout. But anti-war cries did not exhaust the anarcho-punk remit. The movement engaged—sometimes more successfully than others—with feminist, atheist, anti-capitalist and eco-politics. For bands such as Conflict and Flux of Pink Indians, the politics of animal rights, animal liberation, vegetarianism and veganism were central.

Crass's early work ensured that the politics of atheism took a prominent place in the movement's propaganda and artwork. After assembly line workers refused to press copies of the band's first record in protest at the sacrilegious content of the opening song 'Reality Asylum', Crass were obliged to replace the offending article with a silent track—which the band bitterly retitled 'The Sound of Free Speech'. Denunciations of the culpability of organised religion in the persistence of war and human suffering, and attacks on the church's position within the hierarchy of the 'ruling elite', became recurrent themes of the wider movement.

Punk had provided numerous outlets for women performers and feminist messages, but anarcho-punk offered a platform for a distinctively anarcha-feminist politics. Poison Girls combined impassioned invectives against capital and militarism, with sophisticated critiques of the alienated nuclear family, and subtle explorations of gender relations. The women artists and performers within Crass had explored feminist themes since the band's formation, and in 1981 the band released the album *Penis Envy*, conceived as a specifically 'feminist attack', on which only the band's female vocalists appear.[20] The record's lyrical preoccupations were directed as much at the group's predominately male fan base as to the world beyond, driven by an awareness that many of the punks enthused by the driving and aggressive agit-punk that was seen as Crass's stock-in-trade often appeared to find the complexities of gender politics challenging, of secondary concern to the 'more pressing' conflict with the war state, or even an uncomfortable irrelevance.

The complications of Crass's own political position, and by extension that of anarcho-punk, were acute. Explored in the extended essays of Crass's 1982 book *A Series of Shock Slogans and Mindless Token Tantrums*, the politics of anarcho-punk emerge as an interplay between non-violence, counter-culturalism, spartan anti-consumerism and the exploration of personal liberty that might provide the supportive context for a relentless struggle against the forces of capital and the war state. Criticised by some anarchist opponents as a confusion of revolutionary perspectives with the 'politics of lifestyle',[21] anarcho-punk was premised on the adoption of radical practices in the personal lives of its adherents—co-operative and communal living, not-for-profit publishing and artistry, squatting, re-appropriation—that could together help generalise the culture of disobedience and direct action. Throughout, Crass's politics remained an unresolved fusion of the utopian and absolutist, and the acutely personal and immediate.

Crass certainly attacked head-on the assertion that the legitimacy of punk itself rested on its working class origins, and condemned those whose sought to confine participation in punk culture to those who measured up to the bogus criteria of 'street credibility' externally imposed by journalists and music industry pundits.[22] As a critique of the fetishisation of young white male working class street-culture—exemplified by the political schizophrenia of the early 1980s Oi punk wave—and as an attempt to hold open the boundaries of the movement, the argument held great merit. Additionally, anarcho-punk was able to offer something almost entirely absent from the campaigns against rising unemployment of the time—a rudimentary critique of wage-labour itself. In the far less punitive welfare climate of the time, Crass suggested that the young unemployed should reject the passivity of their place in the 'reserve army of labour' and seize the opportunities that freedom from the factory and office afforded them. Celebrated in the band's riotous *Do They Owe Us a Living?*, this was a raucous and uncompromising defence of a new subversive 'giro-ethic'.

There were points, however, at which this rejection of alienated labour found expression in destructively hostile language—in which, for instance, the workers on the Ford production lines were seen as willingly complicit in their own subjugation.[23] And yet, those keen to dismiss anarcho-punk's 'déclassé' politics faced the difficulty that so much of the movement's energies were directed at encouraging collective action against multiple capitalist targets, through language, imagery and song intimately concerned with exposing the social relations of power, ownership and wealth in Thatcher's Britain. By 1984, as many anarcho-punk benefits were concerned with raising money and support for striking miners as for anti-nuclear causes, and the peace movement's conflict with the nuclear state was itself seen as developing an increasingly revolutionary logic. Committed anarcho-punks ran with the hunt saboteurs, whilst denouncing the military and economic imperialism of the USA; they organised public fasts against world hunger, while they prepared clandestine spray-paint attacks on army recruitment offices. What kept the movement connected was the shared subculture of gigs, records and fanzines, not the diktats of any central organising committee, or ultimately the pronouncements of Crass. Anarcho-punk's politics remained a moving target. For critics and supporters alike, even as the movement's manifestos evolved, they remained frustratingly imprecise.

It was a politics that left the movement noticeably separated from both the anti-militarist and anarchist traditions that it initially hoped to fuse. Crass's enthusiasm for some of the venerable institutions of the British pacifist tradition produced some interesting intersections and cultural clashes. Respectable organisations such as the Peace Pledge Union (or in other contexts, the British Union for the Abolition of Vivisection or the National Council for Civil Liberties) found that their postbags were now bursting with envelopes scrawled with garish subversive slogans that revealed letters from young punks eager for the latest news on 'the struggle'. Somewhat taken aback by the attention, the PPU showed little enthusiasm for reflecting the energy or vocabulary of anarcho-punk in any of its materials, preferring to rely on the organisation's time-honoured imagery and language, and side-stepping the punks' feverish appeals for 'anti-war action'. It revealed a mismatch of expectations on both sides.

Of necessity, much of anarcho-punk's political identity was defined in oppositional terms. Crass's profound suspicion at the motivations of the Trotskyist left, ensconced within some of the key campaigning organisations of the day, was in large measure reciprocated by those left activists wary of Crass's anarchist credentials. Crass's association with the Rock Against Racism (RAR) initiative, which many punk bands lent their name to, proved to be short lived, with Crass attacking what they claimed as disingenuous motives of RAR promoters, and the hard-left's hidden agendas.[24] More controversial still was the role of the Anti-Nazi League, and the street-level anti-fascist squads which at that time operated on its fringes. After such a squad arrived uninvited at a Crass gig at London's Conway Hall and began setting about those in the audience with close-cropped or skinhead haircuts (on the assumption that this identified them as fascists), the band were incensed—going on to denounce in song the 'left-wing macho street-fighters willing to kick arse' who revealed their own 'bigotry and blindness' in the process.[25] It served to reinforce the band's anarchist insistence on the parallel between the power aspirations of the hard right and hard left.[26]

The culture of anarcho-punk

The defining visual aesthetic of anarcho-punk was the colour black. Crass maintained that the band had opted to clothe themselves almost entirely in black as a reaction against the 'peacock preoccupations' of the 'fashion punk industry'—to adopt a plain, uniform colour circumvented such 'irrelevances'.[27] When combined with other elements of the band's design and performance, it made them an imposing presence on stage. Many of those drawn to the music and philosophy of Crass soon adopted a similar dress code, refreshing their wardrobes from Army Surplus and charity shops, with cotton-drill and moleskin displacing Levis and leather. At gigs and demonstrations, anarcho-punks sought each other out, in an earlier manifestation of the kind of 'black bloc' seen in today's anti-globalisation protests. Although the similarity of appearance sometimes offered anonymity in the cut and thrust of a lively street march, police forces quickly recognised the hallmark of the new anarchist contingent, and responded accordingly. Critics mused on the apparent irony of 'uniform anarchists' urging the freedom of all from imposed rules (while Crass countered that this was both a trivial observation and a misrepresentation).

And yet, the dress sense of anarcho-punks—however unmissable it remained—was actually one of the least significant aspects of the movement's culture. Far more important was the subcultural expectation of co-operation and self-activity. However partial and halting it proved to be in practice, anarcho-punk was premised on the notion that the movement would sustain and extend its influence through the self-directed activities of its adherents—who would form more bands, produce ever greater numbers of publications, set-up record labels and radical co-operatives, and so generate the cultural infrastructure through which the movement's influence could be multiplied. Although many of those who bought the records and turned out for the gigs ignored the exhortation, there remained a hopeful expectation that anarcho-punks would commit themselves to building the culture of the movement itself, and engage in political activity beyond it. Some anarcho-punks certainly functioned largely as 'fans' of the genre, who bought the music, checked-out the gigs and—subject to sufficient pestering—bought the fanzines, but did little more than act in the role of consumer. Even so, the organisers, promoters, printers, composers, designers and authors of anarcho-punk tended to be thrown up from within the ranks of the movement.

The visual and graphic work of both Gee Sus and Mick Duffield was ground breaking. The disfigured Crass logo; the all-black-clad appearance; the trademark stencil typography, and all the other elements of Crass's graphic packaging offered a striking identity to rival Jamie Reid's work for the Sex Pistols. Sus's stunning artwork of collage and montage gave visceral and graphic reinforcement to Crass's musical messages. Duffield's and Sus's video presentations turned punk gigs into film shows and punctuated Crass's live performance. The work was stunning, and often appalling and horrifying—using juxtaposition, and a fusion of *decollage*, gouache and photo-realist techniques to breathtaking effect.[28] For a band opposed out-right to the commercial packaging and presentation of punk, Crass developed a visual identity that was distinctive and unmistakable. In retro-spect, Sus's work in particular is increasingly recognised as 'having been seminal to the iconography of the "punk generation"'.[29]

Records functioned as another tool in the agit armoury. Covers, defined by their stencil lettering and circular motif, were stripped to black and white, but reconceived as wraparound sleeves—opened up to provide multiple pan-els of information and artwork. Anarcho-punk gigs were also distinguishable from the mainstream commercial circuit in innumerable ways, tending to be organised in youth clubs, scout huts and church halls outside the usual rock circuit, and usually put together by amateur fan promoters. Larger gigs, involving artists such as Crass, Flux of Pink Indians, Conflict or Poison Girls, offered a wide variety of performers: poets with backing tapes, films, drum and vocal duos, alongside full bands. The presentation would be as com-prehensive as possible, as halls would be decked with banners of anarchist and anarcho-punk emblems, TV sets and film screens. There would be no row of bow-tied bouncers on the door; no capitalist promoter in the back-ground; certainly no merchandising stall or hot dog concession; and few incentives for 'ticket touts' to lurk outside. Entrance would be phenomenally cheap and, inevitably, the evening would be a benefit for at least one cause if not several—although the discounted door price might generate fairly meagre receipts. Events got underway the minute the doors opened and were usually wound-up before last buses, tubes and trains so people could get home. These would also be, as they are characterised now, 'all ages show', without access restrictions.[30]

Despite, and partly because of these distinctions from the punk rock norm, anarcho-gigs were vulnerable to attack, and were sometimes marred by outbreaks of violence, usually fairly minor but at other times more seri-ous.[31] In addition to the tensions inherent in anarcho-punk's 'confrontational pacifism', there are a number of other factors that explain this apparent anomaly. As has been mentioned, anarcho-punk's political critique extended to the dominant Trotskyist politics of the hour, and explicitly condemned the highjacking of causes and the manipulation of 'front organisations' by the authoritarian left. At same time, anarcho-punk was implacably hostile to the peripheral far-right and Nazi movements then trying to mobilise in Britain in the context of early Thatcherism. In consequence, anarcho-punk gigs could be seen, by sections of both the hard-left and the far-right, (as well as by thugs or no particular political affiliation), as 'soft targets': the gigs would be found outside the usual club circuit; there would be few security staff able to intervene; and no enthusiasm amongst organisers for summoning the police.[32] On top of that, would-be assailants surmised that the readily identifiable core audience at these gigs subscribed to a form of pacifist politics, which for some included a reluctance even to resort to physical self-defence. Many of the audience were people in their early teens, and—although bands would respond to any violent incidents and protect people as best as they could—in many respects, the audiences were expected to fend for themselves in a culture that, for the most part, frowned on the use of violence. All of which meant that large-scale anarcho-punk gigs were usually characterised by a palpable atmosphere of exhilaration and anticipation—sometimes defiant and celebratory, at other times uncomfortably threatening.

Gigs were also a forum in which innumerable anarcho-punk 'fanzines' would circulate. 'Fanzines' had been a central part of punk culture since titles such as the seminal *Sniffin' Glue* began to document the emerging London punk scene in 1976.[33] As the literary and design equivalent of punk's musical exhortation to 'do-it-yourself', fanzines had become the defining 'xeroxed texts' of the original punk original wave. Self-produced and self-published, the cut-and-paste collage and stencil design ethos of the punk fanzine was enthusiastically taken up by such publications as Rock Against Racism's *Temporary Hoarding* and (to the evident disquiet of some Communist Party officials) the Young Communist League's *Challenge*. Yet, what had effectively begun as a range of amateur publications by young punk music fans was transformed into something more specifically didactic through the experience of anarcho-punk. Often reconceived as 'zines' (to dispense with the associations of the 'fan' prefix) anarcho-punk generated a quite remarkable subterranean network of anarchist publications, which struggled against the design limitations imposed by the now-archaic 'duplicator' presses on which so many were produced to augment the movement's musical output. Direct, uncensored and strident, titles such as *Acts of Defiance*, *Kind Girls*, *No New Rituals*, *Children of the Revolution* and *Pigs Will Fly* used shocking imagery and crude juxtaposition, alongside poetry and song lyrics, to urge the intensification of the struggle against the nuclear state, animal cruelty, unemployment and police harassment. Individual print runs could run into several thousand copies, or be restricted to a few dozen. This entirely uncoordinated and uncatalogued outpouring of young people's radical political writing remained as ephemeral as it was passionate—the turnover of titles proved relentless, and few imprints reached a double-figure issue number—and yet, for a brief while, it provided important confirmation of anarcho-punk's ability to inspire and engage.

Yet this sub-culturally distinct anarcho-punk milieu proved more adept at defining and defending its own independence than in forging effective alliances with other groups recognised as engaged in struggle with a shared set of enemies. Outside of the networks of venues, bands and fanzines, the organisational framework around which the movement might rally its forces remained rudimentary where it existed at all. Crass, reluctant to accept the burdens of political leadership which some in the movement wished them to take on, rarely issued calls for unified action of any sort. Enthusiasts for the spontaneous and the temporary, the band sought to redirect the energies of those keen to be recruited to new anarchist organisations—concerned that the once innovative culture of anarcho-punk risked becoming an impediment of its own.[34] At one point, Crass did set in motion plans for an ambitious mass 'walking tour' of some of the 'key institutions' of the nuclear state—beginning at the Windscale plant, and ending in Parliament Square—intended to demonstrate the movement's political clout. But as the momentum of the initiative grew, and with it the likely scale of the turnout of young, militant punks, Crass reconsidered. Concerned by the possible serious consequences of a series of set-piece confrontations between groups of anarchist punks and the forces of law-and-order, Crass cancelled the event and weathered the resulting criticism. Although the organisational clarity of anarcho-punk never once matched its subcultural distinctiveness, it was still capable of asserting its influence in some of the prominent political and campaign movements of the day.

A list of Crass's own claims to political notoriety in this period would need to include the funding of the promising but short-lived Anarchy Centre in London (a follow-on for the band's support for the defendants in the Persons Unknown trial); high profile opposition to the Falklands War (which led to 'questions in the House' about the band's 'depraved and scurrilous' attack on her majesty's government in the guise of the 'How Does it Feel to be the Mother of a Thousand Dead?' single); and the 'Thatchergate' stunt (a gloriously subversive tape montage of an alleged telephone conversation between Thatcher and Reagan in which the leaders share war plans, which fooled both the FBI and KGB, as well as the British broadsheet press, for many months).[35] Yet behind anarcho-punk's own headline history, lay the countless actions and political initiatives, self-selected by the movement's own adherents, which blossomed uncollated and largely undocumented.

The most striking example of the collective mobilisation of anarcho-punks were the series of anti-capitalist Stop the City (STC) demonstrations in London's financial centre between 1983 and 1984 called to protest 'against war, exploitation and profit' and to 'celebrate life'.[36] Although not initiated solely from within anarcho-punk, Crass's own film documentary of the second STC confirms the extent to which these were primarily, though not exclusively, anarchist and punk affairs.[37] These part-carnivals, part push-and-shove fracas effectively illustrated both the capabilities of the movement and the limitations of its political coherence—demonstrating its disrespect for the routines of traditional law-abiding demonstrations, while at the same time highlighting the movement's uncertainty over questions of strategy and agency.

In their own writing, Crass somewhat overstate the contribution that anarcho-punk made to resuscitating the moribund Campaign for Nuclear Disarmament (CND) in the early 1980s.[38] The initiation of a new arms race, confirmed by plans to deploy first-strike Cruise, Pershing, and SS20 nuclear missiles across Europe, revived anti-nuclear movements across the continent, and would have arisen with or without the intercession of anarcho-punk. What Crass and anarcho-punk can quite legitimately claim is to have convinced a substantial number of radical youth to commit their energies to the most militant anti-militarist wings of the disarmament movement, which laid siege to nuclear installations across the UK and which saw no conflict between its pacifist precepts and its willingness to commit acts of 'criminal damage' on the military property of the nuclear state.

There can also be no question that Crass and anarcho-punk together also reinvigorated the ranks of the once-more marginalised British anarchist movement,[39] which had slid back into the fractious periphery after a brief resurgence in the early 1970s—although the 'old hands' and the 'new punks' never became fully reconciled to one another. Despite the misgivings of some longstanding activists, anarcho-punk both infused the movement with new blood and refashioned its existing pre-occupations the better to reflect the primary concerns of the new militants.

Crass's political position shifted significantly, particularly in the latter years of the band's work (something which could only alter the centre of gravity in the movement as a whole). In the aftershock of the 1982 Falklands War and Thatcher's re-election in 1983, the band began a process of political reassessment that saw the group's commitment to pacifism publicly corrode. The final material produced by the band also indicated the degree to which the 'corporate' position projected by the group since 1977 was beginning to unravel. Typified by the desperate remonstrations of the band's final single 'You're Already Dead' the band were directly castigating the wider peace movement for its own 'appeasement' with the 'war state', and its hesitation at so critical a juncture—the imminent deployment of Cruise missiles. It was the most explicit call to action ever articulated by Crass, and the 'increasingly militant and increasingly covert' trajectory along which the movement was being pointed appeared to be darkening.[40]

The sense of impending catastrophe that came to define Crass's endgame had a number of unintended consequences. The sense of desperation at the inability to defuse the 'ticking time bomb' of nuclear conflagration halted the development of the movement's politics. Shifts in that politics, in part encouraged by the experience of the Miners' Strike, were held in check in the shadow of 'The Bomb'. Such reasoning helped to reinforce the sense of isolation, and indeed siege, preoccupying the movement, and encouraged the development of a distorted sense of its own significance—as if, on its own and unaided, it might yet 'save the world'. Conflict's 1986 album would announce, without a hint of self-parody, that *The Ungovernable Force is Coming*. Yet, the culture of anarcho-punk made the forging of political alliances outside of its own ranks immensely difficult. In that combination of urgency and dread, the anarcho-movement lost perspective and began to substitute itself for the popular uprising it so desperately wanted to see.

The ferocity and intensity of Crass's condemnation of war, the church, the state and 'the system' could prove intoxicatingly attractive to disgruntled and disaffected teenagers, who had already seen in punk rock a way to channel their own rebellious energies, and whose own political perspectives remained fluid. Some of the movement's critics suggested that—despite the informality of anarcho-punk's manifesto—many of its adherents absorbed its messages unreflectively, to become, in effect, 'Crass punks'. There was, they suggested, an unresolved tension between anarcho-punk's advocacy of individual creativity and the political uniformity by which the movement appeared to be defined. Whatever the validity of such a critique, it overlooked what might be seen as a more critical weakness in anarcho-punk's veracity—that many of those intrigued by its musical and cultural passions did not take the movement's political ambitions as seriously, or as literally, as Crass and others around them had hoped. Some were attracted by the music, others by the graphic anti-war imagery, and still others by the subculture's seductive appeal. Many punks turning out for anarcho-punk gigs did not make sharp distinctions between bands such as Crass and other 'commercial' punk acts of which they were also 'fans', and inevitably for many involvement proved to be transitory.

And yet, Crass's fidelity to the principles of independence and self-direction that the band (and the wider movement) took as self-evident, left the critics eager to decry the 'selling-out' of anarcho-punk disappointed. The music and culture of anarcho-punk exposed many tens of thousands of young people to a kaleidoscope of radical ideas and practices, which aimed to stimulate their sense of self-belief, uncluttered by the party-left's fixations with recruitment, bureaucracy and empire building. The fact that Crass, and anarcho-punk as a whole, attracted such intense critical reaction from others within punk should, in many respects, come as no surprise. Crass in particular provided an easy target. By most measures of 'street credibility' they ought not to have registered at all—many of the band were the wrong side of thirty; they were open hippy sympathisers; they lived in a commune in the country and grew their own vegetables; and, on top of that, they had the audacity to get stuck into the punk 'aristocracy'. Not only was their work an explicit critique of the 'for-profit' operation of many other punk outfits; their insistence that punk be recognised as seditious and propagandist infuriated (or left bemused) those who saw punk as the expression of things outrageous, escapist or plain stupid.[41] Punk itself, meanwhile, eluded simple categorisation, proving itself capable of providing the soundtrack to a multiplicity of political projects, from the subtle and jazz-infused 'sex-pol' of the Au Pairs, through the gut socialism of Sham 69 and the UK Subs, the studied art-school Marxism of The Gang of Four, and the makeshift sloganeering of Oi.

Much of the significance and many of the peculiarities of anarcho-punk are revealed in the tensions—some of them 'creative', others of them more problematic—within the movement and its practice. For Crass themselves, such tensions were manifold. There was the sharp contrast between the sophistication, complexity and subtlety of much of the message and the stripped-down, raw directness of the delivery. In every sense, it was not always clear that anarcho-punk's intentions were audible above the noise. Then there was the discord between Crass's irrefutable position as the movement's figureheads and agenda-setters and the band's refusal of that leadership role and reluctance to assume responsibility for it. Crass's own determination to try out different forms of attack, to reinvent their own format and to strain at the creative limits of their project was not always matched in the work of the wider movement, where, in the work of lyric

writers, fanzine editors and graffiti artists, evidence grew of a slide into for-
malism and routine, and where—through familiarity with the subject matters
of war, animal suffering and the nuclear threat—the law of diminishing
returns made itself felt. This was another illuminating conflict—exposing
the contrast between the sophistication of anarcho-punk's analysis of punk
and its betrayals, and the inability of the movement to acknowledge anarcho-punk's own limits, as well as celebrate its strengths.

If Crass and the movement they inspired sought to invest in punk a weight
it could not bear, anarcho-punk remained an unanswerable riposte to the
buffoonery, compromise and squandered principles which had corrupted so
much of punk's original potential. To the tens of thousands of young people who found its intensity inspiring rather than repellent, anarcho-punk
suggested that personal politics, counter-cultural work and 'revolutionary
practice' might once again be the catalyst for a new mass movement for
'peace and freedom'—one which had ultimately eluded the 'rainbow warriors' of an earlier generation. If the ambition went largely unrealised, that
was a fate which most other contemporary 'progressive' movements found
themselves sharing. Crass, at least, saw the challenge as unchanged: 'It's our
world stolen from us every day. We set out to demand it back. Last time they
called us hippies. This time they call us punks.'[42]

Notes

1. See, for instance, G. Arnold, *Kiss This: Punk in the Present Tense* (London, 1997).
2. Radio Caroline reporter 'Mitch', sampled on the Crass LP *Christ—the Album*
   (Crass, 1982).
3. See, for example, E. Echenberg and Mark P., *And God Created Punk* (London,
   1996); A. Boot and C. Salewicz, *Punk: The Illustrated History of a Music Revolution*
   (London, 1996); M. Spitz and B. Mullen, *We Got the Neutron Bomb: The Untold
   Story of LA Punk* (New York, 2001); M. Andersen and M. Jenkins, *Dance of Days:
   Two Decades of Punk in the Nation's Capital* (New York, 2001); *Blank Generation
   Revisited: The Early Days of Punk Rock* (London, 1997); D. Morris, *Destroy*
   (London, 2002); S. Colegrave and C. Sullivan, *Punk* (London, 2001); D. Nolan,
   I Swear I Was There (Bury, 2001) and dozens of other titles.
4. In Jon Savage's now 'classic' general history of British punk, for example, he
   acknowledges his inability to do justice to the phenomenon of Crass and anar-
   chist punk, concluding that due to the complexity of Crass's work 'they
   deserve a book to themselves.' J. Savage, *England's Dreaming: The Sex Pistols and
   Punk Rock* (London, 1991) p.584.
5. These include: G. McKay, 'Crass 621984 ANOK4U2', in G. McKay, *Senseless
   Acts of Beauty: Cultures of Resistance Since the Sixties* (London, 1996) pp.73–101;
   'Postmodernism and the Battle of the Beanfield: British Anarchist Music and

Text of the 1970s and 1980s', in S Earnshaw (ed.), *Postmodern Surroundings* (Amsterdam, 1994) pp.147–66; R. Unterberger, 'Crass' in *Unknown Legends of Rock 'n' Roll* (San Francisco, 1998) pp.259–64.

6. Essays in R. Sabin (ed.), *Punk Rock: So What?* (London, 1999), for instance, contain passing references to the work of Crass, but make no effort to integrate the experience of anarcho-punk into the analytical frameworks on offer.

7. This may begin to change now that members of Crass have begun to publish their own autobiographical and retrospective work, notably: P. Rimbaud, *Shibboleth: My Revolting Life* (Edinburgh, 1998); and G. Vaucher, *Crass Art and Other Pre Post-Modernist Monsters* (Edinburgh, 1999).

8. Crass, *The Feeding of the 5,000* (Small Wonder, 1978).

9. 'Punk is Dead', *The Feeding of the 5,000*.

10. Sex Pistols, *God Save the Queen* (Virgin, 1977).

11. J. Savage, *England's Dreaming*, pp.355–9; Julian Temple (director), The Filth and the Fury (UK, 2000); P. Rimbaud, 'The Last of the Hippies', *A Series of Shock Slogans and Mindless Token Tantrums* (London, 1982) p.62.

12. P. Rimbaud, *Shibboleth*, pp.36–68.

13. Crass, '…In Which Crass Voluntarily "Blown Their Own"', insert with the retrospective Crass LP *Best Before 1984* (Crass Records, 1984).

14. 'Still Ignorant, not so Crass', *Living Marxism*, February 1999; P. Rimbaud, *Shibboleth*, p.259; 'Preface', Crass: *Love Songs* (Hebden Bridge, 2004); p.xxviii; Crass, '…In Which'.

15. Crass's own contemporary accounts of the development of the band and the anarcho-punk movement can be found in Crass, *A Series of Shock Slogans and Mindless Tokens Tantrums* (London, 1982); and Crass, '…In Which'.

16. *Tongue In Cheek*, No 2, n.d. but circa mid-1982.

17. Rimbaud, 'Preface', *Love Longs*, p.xxiv.

18. Crass, '…In Which Crass'.

19. 'Demoncrats', *Stations of the Crass* (Crass Records, 1981).

20. Crass, *Penis Envy* (Crass Records, 1981).

21. See, for instance, the features on Crass and Poison Girls in *Anarchy*, no.34, n.d., but circa 1982.

22. Music journalist Garry Bushell—a persistent and vocal critic of the band and of anarcho-punk—repeatedly attacked Crass for proposing such views. See, for example, 'The Mystic Revelation of Crasstafari', *Sounds*, 30 August 1980.

23. The lyrics of Crass's 'End Result', from *The Feeding of the 5,000*, conclude: 'I hate the living dead and their work in the factories / They go like sheep to their production lines / They live on illusions, don't face the realities / All they live for is that big blue sign / It says…Ford.'

24. See Crass, '…In Which Crass'; *A Series of Shock Slogans*.

25. Crass, 'White Punks on Hope', *Stations of the Crass* (Crass Records, 1979).

26. See the discussion in, P. du Noyer, 'At Cross Purposes', *New Musical Express*, 14 February 1981.

27. See for instance M. Holderness, 'Crass', *Peace News*, 18 May 1979; P. Rimbaud,

'Preface', *Love Songs*; 'Still Ignorant, not so Crass'.

28. See G. Vaucher, *Crass Art and Other Pre Post-Modernist Monsters*; and all Crass record sleeves and artwork. Sus now works under her real name, Vaucher.

29. 'Artist profile: Gee Vaucher', 96 Gillespie Gallery, London: http://96gillespie.com/artists_profiles/vaucher.htm (accessed 20 April 2004).

30. These latter aspects—'all ages access' and public transport-friendly finish times are familiar enough features in today's music scenes, but they were significant breaks with the dominant rock'n'roll conventions of the day. For an evocative account of a 1981 Crass, Poison Girls, and Flux of Pink Indians gig at the 100 Club, London, see E. Pouncey, 'Tea and Anarchy', *Sounds*, 20 June 1981.

31. The fraught and atmosphere of a volatile and sporadically violent Crass gig (Perth, Scotland, 4 July 1981) is captured on the CD: Crass, *You'll Ruin it for Everyone* (Pomona Records, 1983).

32. Rimbaud describes the attack on an early Conway Hall, London Crass audience by leftists seeking 'Nazi scum' in *Shibboleth*, p.119: 'Anyone with hair shorter than half an inch…was regarded as fair game. The resultant carnage was ugly, unnecessary and utterly indefensible.'; and other attacks by right and left, p.127.

33. See the collected *Sniffin' Glue* (London, 2000).

34. P. Rimbaud, 'Preface', *Love Songs*, p.xix.

35. See 'Crass Statement', *Freedom*, 27 November 1982; '…In Which Crass'; P. Rimbaud, Shibboleth, pp.250–4.

36. Leaflets and posters advertising 'Stop the City' events, 1983–84, in author's possession.

37. Crass and Exitstencil Films, *Stop the City 29–03–84* (*Rough Cut, August 1984*), (Crass, 1984).

38. J. Savage, *England's Dreaming*, p.584; P. Rimbaud, *Shibboleth*: 'our efforts on the road slowly bought CND back to life', p.109.

39. J. Savage, *England's Dreaming*, p.584.

40. P. Rimbaud quoted in N. Perry and H. Fielder, 'Crass: A Militant Tendency?', *Sounds*, 25 October 1986.

41. For an exploration of such views of punk, see S. Home, *Cranked Up Really High: Genre Theory and Punk Rock* (Code X, Hove) 1995.

42. P. Rimbaud, 'The Last of the Hippies', *A Series of Shock Slogans*, p.63.

The Rise and Fall of the Labour League of Youth

Michelle Webb

On 8 May 1923, at the annual conference of Labour women, Dr Marion Phillips proposed a resolution urging the Labour Party to form a young people's section to give 'prominence to the pleasures of an outdoor life and to anti-militaristic teaching'.[1] The outcome was the appointment of a sub-committee and a circular issued in August 1924, 'organisation of youth', which initiated the Labour Party youth movement. Two years later it became the Labour League of Youth (LLY), which remained its title until its demise in 1959. Throughout its time, the League produced a host of prominent political figures and, of equal importance, the unsung foot soldiers of the Labour Party who over several decades voluntarily offered their services in political activity at local branch and council level.

The Labour Party did not intend that its youth sections should exist as separate organisations. Rather, it was recommended that the 'organisation of youth should become part of the ordinary organising work of the party, in order that they should more readily and enthusiastically take their place in the labour movement as they reach adult years'. No alteration to the party constitution was deemed necessary, though young people were to be given 'the right means of co-operating in the general work of the constituencies, without forcing upon them responsibilities and duties which should only be borne by the organisations of adult members of the party'.[2]

The scheme under which the Labour youth organisation was established set membership between the ages of fourteen and twenty-one with an annual subscription of 6d. Each section elected its own management committee from its members. In addition, the general committee of the constituency party made its own appointments to the youth section's management committee, typically including a representative from the divisional women's section. The general committee representatives would, it was felt, 'enable the work of the young to be closer co-ordinated with that of the party and also would enable the young members to have the guidance of people more experienced in the party's work' The youth section could, in turn, appoint two members to represent it on the constituency party's general committee, although they were not allowed to vote. From the beginning there was concern that full representation might lead to 'exploitation by either side whenever a disagreement existed in the party', or to the youth sections having the final decision in the selection of a party election candidate. If there was a desire by any young member to exercise their full rights then the adult men's and women's sections of the divisional party were open to membership to those aged sixteen and over.[3]

The scope and objectives of the fledgling youth movement were initially the subject of much attention by the party's National Executive Committee (NEC). In 1924, it was agreed that the three main areas of interest for youth sections should be recreation, education and electioneering. Prominence was to be given to encouraging and developing the interest of the young and sections were instructed 'not to over-emphasise their political side'. For those under the age of fourteen activities were to be of a largely 'recreational character' and no special plans were made to bring them into contact with the 'political side of the movement'.[4] Steady progress was reported with 150 branches in 1925 rising to 206 the following year, a trend that continued throughout the 1930s. In 1934, a year of 'greater activity than in any previous year and progress reported everywhere', there was a significant increase in the number of branches from 263 to 492. During the Second World War many branches disappeared but a revived youth organisation peaked at just over 800 branches in 1951, before declining again thereafter. Although accurate figures for individual membership do not exist, branch memberships could vary from twenty to 200 members at any particular time. By 1929, the League began to develop a more complex regional and national structure with advisory committees and federations established to co-ordinate activities between local branches and the first annual League conference was held that year.[5]

During its existence the LLY provided a rich social, educational and political outlet for young people and a valuable election resource for the party. This article seeks to explore the activities and experiences of those who passed through the ranks of the LLY, examining the relationship of the adult party to this resource and the extent to which membership of the league was seen as an 'apprenticeship' for future political activities and careers in the Labour Party. Using oral testimony, it hopes to illustrate the potentially vibrant social and political life as well as the conflicts and challenges available to those young people committed to the Labour Party.

Parent and child

The relationship between the Labour Party and its junior members in the League of Youth was in some ways analogous to that of a parent and child. There was a genuine desire to nurture the young, to educate them in the ways of the older family members, and to allow them to try out certain 'adult roles' from time to time. There would, however, be many occasions when the child fell foul of its parent by pushing the boundaries too far and have to be reminded of the house rules. Eric Ryder, a prominent member of the Huddersfield LLY, echoed this interpretation when speaking at an LLY meeting in 1933 on relations between the league and party. The LLY should hold to the adage that 'children should be seen and not heard', as they were not— in his opinion—yet in a position to discuss party policy.6 Speaking at the 1937 party conference, Theresa Gorringe, the delegate for the Wandsworth divisional party and former member of the London advisory committee of the LLY, believed that the party attitude could be summed up as 'Go and find out what the League of Youth is doing and tell them not to!'7

Clearly the relationship between the LLY and its parental organisation was, like many family relationships, often difficult. The August 1933 edition of the league's *New Nation* quoted Goethe that: 'The destiny of any nation at any given time depends on the opinions of its young people under five and twenty' but 'elders and betters' rarely accept such opinions.[8] A basic strain in the relationship between the party and its youth groups was evident with regard to the definition of youth itself: what was to be the upper-age limit allowed for membership of the LLY? Initially eligible members were those aged between fourteen and twenty-one. In 1927, however, the age-limit was raised to twenty-five on condition that membership of the party was also taken up at this point. Even so, many stayed on unofficially beyond their time. Gilbert Hanson, a Labour veteran until his death in 2002, was fondly remembered for being the 'oldest youth member' in the Huddersfield branch. Gilbert argued that you could not possibly have a youth movement with an upper age limit of twenty-one, as political views were not then sufficiently formed or mature.[9] Similarly, a delegate from the Leeds Labour Party speaking at the party conference in 1933 claimed that the most active members of the LLY in the north tended to be over the age of twenty-five. It was, he said, 'the years between 25 and 30 [that] bring with them a certain maturity which the League of Youth presently lacks'.[10] Nonetheless, the same year saw a resolution to raise the LLY age limit to thirty defeated by conference as the benefits to the party of such added 'maturity' were unclear.

The NEC sought to use age as a tool to control the activities of its mem-

bers. Thus, the NEC's concern that the upper age of LLY delegates to conference would give rise to the possibility of dual representation eventually
led to an alteration of the party rules. From January 1938, LLY members
aged twenty-five would resign their League membership by the end of that
year and, by 1939, those aged twenty-one would do the same. This ruling
proved contentious. At the 1936 party conference, a delegate from Ealing
opposed the changes on the grounds that it was those members aged
between twenty-one and twenty-five who had been instrumental in setting
up the LLY in the first place and now they were old enough to both advise
younger members and maintain contact with the 'adult' party.[11] Conversely,
some younger members themselves objected to domination by the older
comrades within the LLY. Jean Tait from Glasgow, addressing a league conference in 1936, claimed to be horrified at the 'bald heads' sitting in front
of her. 'If it is traditional and acceptable to be married at sixteen', she asked,
'then how could anyone have the audacity to believe they are still young at
25?'[12] Ultimately, the party was concerned that added years would lead to
increased politicisation, encouraging demands for a more powerful and independent role being sought by younger members of the party. For this reason
the NEC remained unmoved, as did the new upper-age limit of twenty-one.

Parental control was also maintained in other ways. The LLY constitution
was peppered with checks and balances, which became more rigid over time.
It was clear from the outset that the principal purpose of a Labour youth
movement—insofar as the party centre was concerned—was to act as an
enrolment agency for Labour. The LLY was to attract young people who,
drawn in by the vibrant social and educational activities on offer, would ded-
icate their unstinting loyalty and support to the party and its policies. In
recognition of this, the party was very cautious with regard to the level and
extent of the LLY's political commitments. On the other hand the league was
itself an organisation with a rising membership that wanted to extend its influence and take a more active role in policy-making. The very fact that the 'adult'
party wrote the constitution and the rulebook, and controlled the LLY purse-
strings, left its younger members in no doubt where the real power lay.

This was certainly the view held by Peter and Doreen Wallace, Labour
activists in Huddersfield. Looking back on his time in the LLY in the late
1940s and early 1950s, Peter felt that youth had 'a restricted role to play in
the Labour Party', and sensed that the constituency party did not want a youth
section at all. He and his comrades felt 'surplus to requirements' and 'unnecessary' until the elections came around. Doreen agreed, though had to admit
that the league provided 'a damned good social club between elections'.[13]
Similar concerns were raised elsewhere. Tom Megahy, former MEP for West

Yorkshire, had chaired the Scottish League of Youth in Lanark in the early fifties, while his wife Jean, whom he met in the LLY, was a founder member of the Mirfield branch. Speaking some years later, Tom recalled constant conflict between the radical views of the LLY and the party, particularly when Labour was in government. Jean, too, recalled allowing herself, naively, to be drawn into a peace group as a youth member, only to find herself threatened with expulsion from the party should she continue the activity.[14]

The party's restrictions of the activities of the LLY raised concerns that the youth movement was falling some way short of its full potential. By as early as 1927, many party conference delegates felt that the disproportionate attention to LLY branches was harming other Labour initiatives such as the Trade Union Defence Campaign and the Agricultural Campaign; a feeling that was compounded when a special league conference was cancelled due to lack of money.[15] While there was no shortage of ideas as to how the LLY could increase its membership, these were often ignored. In 1928, a request for an autonomous national youth organisation was rejected on the grounds that with a general election imminent, the party would be better served by its youth remaining in close association with its constituencies. Even so, the delegate for Wood Green and Southgate suggested a one-day rally to halt the waste of youth resources and Ernest Bevin warned that if the party was not willing to finance its youth movement adequately, then it would fall prey to industrialists or other employers who were able to use their money to influence potential Labour support.[16] Such concerns were a recurrent theme throughout the 1930s and 1940s. In 1933, Harry Wickham of the Buckingham District Labour Party insisted that 'without youth there will be no socialist majority. Youth is needed in the party and the trade unions.' Will Nally of the Mossley Labour Party argued that 'youth is the most precious possession of the socialist movement'.[17]

Despite regular expressions of frustration, the Labour Party did develop its youth section in the 1930s. A youth organiser, Maurice Webb, was appointed in 1933, and a member of the LLY was also nominated to sit on the NEC (although without voting powers). The party agreed to league requests to establish a monthly newspaper—*New Nation*—to replace its monthly bulletin. In 1934 the Clarion Youth Campaign was established from which emerged a 'squad' that sold copies of *New Nation* on the streets 'shoulder to shoulder' and directly challenging those selling *Fascist Weekly* and *Blackshirt*.[18]

The LLY had from its first conference in 1929 demanded, with increasing insistence, that it become an autonomous body able to discuss and formulate party policy and register decisions via conference resolutions. Many members had, after all, been endorsed as parliamentary candidates and some were already on borough councils. Nevertheless, the NEC consistently rejected such a move as being 'fatal, both to the interests of the League and to this party'. While, as noted above, some concessions had been given to the LLY and the party had affiliated on the LLY's behalf to a number of organisations, including the Socialist Youth International, under its 'model rules', advisory committee of the LLY were not allowed to 'deal with matters relating to the constitution or party policy'. According to Arthur Jenkins, the league's representative on the NEC: 'There can only be one authority in this movement, if ever it is going to be effective, for coming to decisions on party policy, and that is this conference'.[19]

The party was concerned that political opinions within the LLY might diverge from the official policy. By the mid-1930s the NEC believed that many Labour youth members were spending too much of their time criticising the party instead of organising their own affairs within the League. The real object of the LLY, as stated in a 1936 NEC memorandum on youth, should be to 'enrol large numbers of young people and by a social life of its own provide opportunities for people to study party policy and to give loyal support to the party of which they are members'.[20] By this time, moreover, the NEC was convinced that the LLY had become susceptible to communist influence. The 1936 LLY conference passed a resolution in favour of a 'united front' with the Communist Party of Great Britain (CPGB). In response the NEC decided to disband the LLY's National Advisory Committee (NAC), cancel the conference due to be held the following Easter, and suspend *New Nation*, in which LLY members were airing their views. 'Throughout the conference', the report records, 'the Young Communist League were represented in the gallery and maintained contact with delegates on the floor of the conference, including certain members of the [NAC]'. Despite imposing these changes, the NEC insisted that it remained 'as anxious as ever for the development of a strong youth section of the party, based upon loyalty to the party and its conference decisions' and instructed the LLY to reorganise itself in accordance with the new rules set out for it by the NEC.[21]

The LLY did not passively accept the NEC's parental discipline, although it was effectively powerless to resist. Cyril Lacey, chair of the LLY advisory committee in 1936, acknowledged that the movement was set up largely on a social and recreational basis, but he suggested that the NEC had not taken the impact of economic changes since 1929 into account. Unemployment and 'blind-alley' jobs had politicised youth, he informed the party conference, leaving them to look for a political basis from which to operate. If the terms of reference were too rigid within the Labour Party, he warned, then the youth would look elsewhere. The delegate for Garnsworth put it more bluntly: 'If the NEC want to run the League of Youth like a glorified Sunday School then it simply will not attract youth.' He believed that if the young were deemed fit to be sent to war then they had the right to self-determination as a movement.[22]

The enforced disbandment of the league's leadership structures and its reorganisation under new, more stringent, rules, combined with the impact of the Second World War from 1939, had a dire effect Labour's youth membership. By 1945, only a handful of branches remained in existence, the LLY executive had been wound up, and the party youth officer did not return to his post. Eventually, renewed interest followed Labour's 1945 general election victory. Youth officers, consultative and advisory committees were again put in place, membership increased, and the number of LLY branches reached a post-war high of just over 800 in 1951. By the late 1950s, however, there had set in a swathe of negative feeling towards the NEC in its response to both recruitment and retention, a point perhaps best indicated at the 1959 Labour conference, whereat the national youth officer, Alan Williams, attended as a visitor and not a delegate.[23] From 1955 to the end of the decade, the number of branches declined along with LLY membership. Although Hugh Gaitskell appointed a Youth Commission in 1959 to examine the wider implications of youth, the results were obscured by the subsequent general election.[24]

In 1932, in the *League of Youth Bulletin*, a member posed the pessimistic question, 'Is the League of Youth Dying?'[25] There is no doubt that the determination of the party to keep its youth out of party policy and the equal determination of its young members to be involved was a constant source of conflict. For all Labour's parental discipline, however, the LLY did not completely die and grew again out of the ashes after the war. The reasons for this survival are several, and are considered below.

Politics and fresh air

Recreation and education were important elements of life in the LLY and together left the average member with little time for other things. Both were well supported by the party and both are prominent in the recollections of former LLY members. The constant round of activity led to efforts by members to establish a permanent home for their respective LLY branches. John Kotz, a founder member of South Hackney LLY, recollects with enthusiasm the Hoddeston Socialist Youth Hostel, later known as the Clarion Youth Hostel. Perhaps the only one of its kind, it was established by London members of the pre-war LLY whose unemployment benefit was supplemented by a grant from Sir Stafford Cripps to renovate a semi-derelict house in Ware, north-east of London. The hostel had its own management committee and warden. Two meetings were held each week with an average of thirty members in attendance. 'Down the Clarion', John remembered, 'we lived as socialists'.[26] In October 1933, H. V. Tewson, assistant secretary of the TUC, visited the hostel to speak on the 'structure of trade unionism', and spoke to *New Nation* about how greatly impressed he was with this group of young people. 'Youth—as keen as mustard. Youth—alive. Youth—a potential font of energy…' He went on to say that he wished there were another hundred centres like it.[27] Sadly, the building was later placed under a compulsory purchase order to make way for industrial development.

Similar schemes to provide premises suitable for meetings and leisure activities were to be found in other parts of the country. In 1929, the Southgate branch took over a disused army hut, which they turned into headquarters complete with sports ground and pavilion. The same year, Normanton and Altoft acquired rooms adequate enough to house a separate club for boys and girls and a gym club.[28] Gilbert Hanson, a member of the Huddersfield branch in the late 1940s and early 1950s, can remember helping to lay the dance floor at the rooms they rented in Station Street, something that seemed a 'natural thing to do' for unemployed people with time on their hands.[29] The focus on leisure activities was encouraged by the Labour Party through its affiliation to organisations such as the Youth Hostel Association and the National Workers' Sports Association. Both provided the LLY with access to a wide range of sporting activities, indoor and outdoor.

Many of the social activities offered by the LLY were designed to make opportunities to meet other young people. In 1929 London branches held a summer camp on the edge of Ashdown Forest, which was advertised to other branches for a fee of 15 shillings, and including the rail fair. Shoreditch joined Southgate's open day and made their way through the streets of 'this respectable Conservative neighbourhood wearing red Tam O'Shanter hats and gold tassels, clearly indicating to which party they belonged'. Bedford ran a river trip with a picnic open to all.[30] By 1931, weekend camping trips were being initiated, with Hugh Dalton opening the first permanent weekend camp in London.

The arts also played a prominent role in league activities. Plays—sometimes for pure entertainment, often for political propaganda purposes—were put on around the country. Peter Sykes can remember being chosen for the leading part of the three-act play put on by the LLY in Huddersfield.[31] John Kotz, too, recalled the Unity Theatre visiting his LLY branch, while members of the group organised play-reading sessions.[32]

At all times, the attention and scrutiny by the party was never far away. Given that LLY members were effectively serving their political apprenticeships, even the running of routine activities such as whist drives were watched carefully. Maurice Hackett noted that most branches were running their own drives by 1929, and was concerned that care should be taken in moving players and checking scores so as not to bring the game into disrepute. It was suggested that LLY branches follow 'the system of moves, trumps, indication, checking, etc favoured by the party drives'.[33]

The LLY was not merely a social organisation. 'The joy of combining propaganda with pleasure' was how Eric Fisher described the linking of rambling and cycling with open-air meetings, leafleting and canvassing.[34] Betty Boothroyd, now the retired speaker of the House of Commons, was another LLY member who saw the link between the social and political aspects of the LLY. In her autobiography, she includes a photograph of herself with league members on Haworth Moor, describing it as 'politics and fresh air'.[35] Jimmy Allan shared such sentiments. Jimmy, known to many of his comrades as 'Red Allan' and the only surviving member of a family of six children whose father had died in the Great War, began rambling with the LLY in the early 1930s at the age of sixteen, and continues to do so today. Rambling became the love of Jimmy's life, marred only by the death of his walking partner and wife Audrey whom he met in the LLY. Unemployment took him and his friends to the hills. As a group of men—plumbers, painters, and joiners—all out of work but sharing a common interest, they were used to long walks with sandwiches in pocket, looking for work. With little else to do, they formed their political views on the moors over Huddersfield and further afield.[36]

But political apprenticeships also necessitated more cerebral activity. Writing in 1929, Eric Fisher believed like many others that the acquisition of knowledge was the key to power and that the young should be 'thrashing out the problems of modern Britain' week by week with discussion groups, guest speakers and study classes. Only by the sparks lit by such groups, he insisted, would 'the mighty flame of socialism continue to burn and spread'; only with an 'educated democracy' would Labour as a movement be successful.[37] To give substance to such claims, one of the objects of the LLY as defined in its model rules was to:

> provide study circles, classes and debates in order to give understanding of the conduct of public work in association with the Labour Party…Apart from amusement, discussions on party policy, and classes in connection with the same, are not only allowable, but encouraged.[38]

By 1935, 116 study groups had been set up around the country.

The LLY was also affiliated to the National Council of Labour Colleges (NCLC) by the 1930s, the primary function of which was for 'the education of workers from the working class point of view, through the medium of colleges, classes and public lectures; the co-ordination and extension of this independent working class educational work; the issuing of leaflets, syllabuses, etc, for the assistance of class tutors and students'.[39] Affiliation meant that each LLY branch was entitled to free access to classes and one free correspondence course each year. A 1933 NCLC advertisement in *New Nation* stated: 'He will be a smart policeman who will arrest the spread of ideas, but apathetic Labourists do it daily.'[40] Remembering the guest speakers and lecturers from the NCLC, John Kotz said that he owed 'a lot to the League of Youth in my education', and continued, echoing many other members of working-class youth organisations in the inter-war period, by saying that he had 'a better education in the League of Youth than at school'.[41]

Various Labour publications, listed the books deemed to be essential reading for the budding socialist: Blatchford, Shaw, Cole, Lansbury and others who embodied the early socialism of the Labour Party. There was also the ILP Bookshop, the Left Book Club and the Fabian Library, which held at any one time about 5000 volumes. LLY branches were able, as an organisation, to subscribe and, for a fee of ten shillings a month, borrow a box of twenty books for a period of three months. Indeed, South Hackney LLY established the 'Red Circle Circulating Library', which included socialist and literary works that they hoped would also attract non-socialists.

It is difficult to gauge the extent to which the LLY shaped the political views of its members. The movement was predominantly working-class with its fair share of unemployed members. Many had a family background of political involvement or support for the Labour tradition. Jimmy Allan, at ninety years old, did almost the whole of the interview with the author from a standing position, stopping only briefly to make a cup of tea, having apparently lost nothing of the urge to deliver a speech from a soapbox. Jimmy has been a Labour member for over seventy years, although his involvement with both the co-operative movement and trade unionism means that he identifies himself more as a member of the labour movement than of simply the Labour Party. Jimmy and his friends decided that as individuals they were weak, but as a group they stood a chance; it was to this end that the Huddersfield branch of the LLY was formed in the early 1930s. Allan saw himself as a propagandist and agitator, prepared to be out on the street for any cause. Anti-fascism marches, aid for China and Spain, May Day rallies, anti-war marches—'any chance and you were out on the streets'. He can remember carrying a hand bell and chair around the streets and delivering a sermon until moved on either by the police or the neighbours.[42] An LLY education was evidently something to be shared.

A marvellous experience

The political apprenticeship supplied by the LLY was integral to many who went on to pursue active political careers. Betty Boothroyd described her experience in the LLY as providing her with a 'passport to a lifetime in politics and public service', and recalled the fun of meeting people of her own age in the League. It was through the LLY that she attended study courses and lectures laid on by the party, thereby providing a 'first experience in front-line politics—and [she] relished it'.43 Lord Judd, too, who followed his sister Nan into the LLY, gained much from his position as vice-chair and later 'prime minister' in the local Youth Parliament.44 Similarly, Granville Whiteley, a member of Huddersfield LLY after the Second World War, believed he would not have entered politics without the experiences he had in the LLY. The league's socialist views were identical to his and gave him the opportunity to meet people and organise them, the two things he enjoyed most. Certainly, his wife Barbara (also a member) recalls Granville's ability to 'get people to do things'. Barbara believed the LLY helped form her opinions, as prior to her membership she held few political views. Following meetings she would find herself arguing with her father, a Liberal, and him asking, 'Where have you got that idea from?'45 For Gilbert Hanson, meanwhile, life in the Huddersfield LLY (which he chaired in 1949) was a means by which to have input into the Labour Party and the social activities were a welcome but secondary concern. Hanson saw the LLY as a mainstream option, offering a voice and influence within the party that groups on the far left would never have.46

Finally, if an apprenticeship was needed for electioneering, then it was undoubtedly served by those LLY members who learnt from their elders, tricks of the trade they would never forget. Tom Megahy, for example, recalled league members being used to fill in the gaps when candidates or guest speakers from the party had not yet arrived. Trying to retain the interest and attention of a waiting crowd or being placed on a platform at short notice to move a vote of thanks was 'a marvellous experience in public speaking' and one which paid dividends in 1952 when he was selected to represent Scotland in Leeds for the finals of a debating competition, sponsored by the *Daily Herald*.[47]

The LLY provided two generations of young people with a rich social life and an outlet for political views and activities in an era when young people had to make their own entertainment. The members themselves, with only their own organisational skills and little money, successfully managed the day-to-day running of the LLY branches. Yet two generations, growing up in different political, economic and social climates, both saw their youth movements disbanded.

An inherent weakness in the long-term viability of the movement was that the initiative to establish a meaningful organisation came from youth itself (with the support of the women's movement), and was not wholeheartedly embraced by the Labour Party. By 1959 then Labour leader Hugh Gaitskell had come to the conclusion that young people were 'repelled by what they feel to be the fusty, old-fashioned, working class attitudes of the people who run the Labour Party'. The paradox he addressed was 'how can we meet the demands of these young people without seeming to betray all the ideals of the old people?'[48]

In his biography of Gaitskell, Philip Williams states that the lavish attention paid to the LLY was one of Gaitskell's most distinctive features. In his very first speech, Gaitskell talked of the need for fresh thinking, which could only come from the younger members. It was, however, in the young people themselves that Gaitskell showed the most interest; he went on their rambles and joined them in their Sunday classes discussing socialism. Williams believes that Gaitskell wished to educate the young in the values of socialism but believed that the main party was the proper arena for the development of policy and political decision-making. He could see the factional disputes developing in the youth movement and knew that party officers would sooner or later stamp on the enthusiasm as had been done in the late 1930s. With this in mind, Gaitskell saw the development of youth groups as organisations separate from the party from which there would be a clear transition to the adult body. The LLY was not in any way seen as an organisational springboard, but rather as a diversion from mainstream party politics.

The Labour Party, for its part, acted as a responsible parent, keeping a firm hand on the purse strings, frequently reminding the young how they were financed. It provided the legal framework and guidance, and put in place officers to monitor the processes and progress of the groups. Fearing infiltration from the left and while in government, when in Gilbert Hanson's view it was trying to look respectable, the party did not want a youth movement acting as the tail wagging the dog.[49] In reality it would be difficult to imagine that the public would take the enthusiasm and rebelliousness of youth at their own conference more seriously than the party's own soberly arrived at resolutions and policies.

By 1955 Alice Bacon and other Labour leaders with responsibility for the league were of the view that the NEC had done its best for the LLY and that any further action would have been half-hearted. Bacon believed that the national organisation had become 'a super structure without any foundation'.[50] By the 1959s, Labour had suffered three successive general election defeats and part of the accepted explanation was the party's declining appeal to young people. One of the outcomes of this realisation was the re-examination of the party's organisation relationship with its youth, out of which process subsequently emerged the Young Socialists.

In 1961 Richard Crossman remarked in his diary on 'Labour's failure to organise a youth movement'. He was impressed by the knowledge and excited responses of young protesters towards South Africa's Apartheid regime, the contrast with the lack of such activity in the party as 'one of the reasons we fail with young people'.[51] Revolutionary passions, as Hobsbawm would argue, 'are more common at eighteen than at 35'.[52] Youth, by its very nature, was and will always be prone to rebelliousness and left-wing politics, especially in the hands of idealistic youth will inevitably be critical of the establishment. Given such circumstances, it was difficult to see a future for a Labour youth movement with no official powers. New ways of thinking were needed. Ultimately, the jagged edges of war, unemployment and 'blind-alley' jobs were being smoothed by affluence and the party proved unable to catch up.

Notes

1. Labour Party, *Report of the Annual Conference of the Labour Party* [hereafter RACLP], 1923, pp.60–5.
2. 'Organisation of Youth', RACLP, 1924, pp. 2–5.
3. RACLP, 1924.
4. RACLP, 1924.
5. RACLP, 1933, p.34.
6. Minutes of Huddersfield Labour League of Youth, August 1933 (Huddersfield University Library).
7. RACLP, 1937, p.223.
8. *New Nation*, August 1933.
9. Gilbert Hanson, Huddersfield, interview with author 18 November 2002.
10. RACLP, 1933, pp.216–17.
11. RACLP, 1936.
12. RACLP, 1937, p.222.

13. Peter and Doreen Wallace, Huddersfield, interview with author, 13 November 2002.
14. Tom and Jean Megahy, Mirfield, interview with author, 16 November 2002.
15. RACLP, 1927.
16. RACLP, 1928, pp.161–2.
17. RACLP, 1933, pp.147–8.
18. RACLP, 1934.
19. RACLP, 1936, p.238.
20. RACLP, 1936.
21. RACLP, 1936.
22. RACLP, 1936.
23. RACLP, 1959.
24. RACLP, 1959.
25. *League of Youth Bulletin*, September 1932.
26. John Kotz, Suffolk, interview with author, 27 May 2003.
27. *New Nation*, October 1933.
28. *League of Youth Bulletin*, 1929.
29. Gilbert Hanson, interview.
30. *League of Youth Bulletin*, July 1929.
31. Peter Sykes, Huddersfield, interview with author, 13 November 2002.
32. John Kotz, interview.
33. *League of Youth Bulletin*, September 1929.
34. RACLP, 1929.
35. Boothroyd, *The Autobiography* (London, 2002.) pp.76–7.
36. Jimmy Allan, Huddersfield, interview with author, 29 November 2002
37. *League of Youth Bulletin*, September 1929.
38. *League of Youth Bulletin*, February 1931.
39. NCLC from collection of J. P. M. Millar, General Secretary. (http://www.aim25.ac.uk/cgi-bin/search2?coll_id=5906&inst_id=1)
40. *New Nation*, 1933.
41. John Kotz, interview.
42. Jimmy Allan, interview.
43. Boothroyd, *Autobiography*, pp.2, 44.
44. Lord (Frank) Judd, House of Lords, letter to author, 27 April 2003.
45. Granville and Barbara Whiteley, Huddersfield, interview with author, March 2003.
46. Gilbert Hanson, interview.
47. Tom Megahy, interview.
48. P.L. Williams, *Hugh Gaitskell: A Political Biography* (London, 1979), p.388.
49. Gilbert Hanson, interview.
50. RACLP, 1955.
51. J. Morgan (ed.), *The Backbench Diaries of Richard Crossman* (London, 1981). p. 940.
52. E. Hobsbawm, *Age of Extremes: The Short Twentieth Century, 1914–91* (London, 1995), p.298.

Memory, Youth, Hope
Features of youth activism in the last years of apartheid

Jonathan Grossman

Ten years ago, one of the many 'births' of the new South Africa coincided with the development of the musical genre now known as kwaito. A recent industry analysis into the 'kwaito generation' highlighted (to a presumed doubting public) the market opportunities, the aspirational career and entre-preneurial possibilities, and the consumer strength, of the kwaito generation.[1] Even the routine possibilities of youth music as youth counter-culture have been anaesthetised by the increasingly dominant vision of the 'dictates of the market' to which youth should be striving to conform and against whose benchmarks they are to be measured—and found wanting. Moulding youth in the terms of the market, the benchmark of what should be achieved, is necessarily denigrating the majority of youth who do not mea-sure up. The same approach is used, *ex post facto*, to portray and characterise the youth and their struggles and place in struggles of the past. Underpinned by an ideologised myth of convergence between capital and the masses in struggle against apartheid, history is systematically being reconstructed into a unilinear progression towards that convergence and the class-collaboration partnerships between capital and labour of the present.[2]

Commenting on the school matriculation results of 2003, the Minister of Education said they showed youth continuing to move 'from the despair and loneliness of the past to the hope and prosperity of the future'.[3] Indications are that only five per cent of the youth passing the exam would find employ-ment in the formal economy. For many of the remaining youth, the progress about which the minister enthused is likely to be characterised by movement from unemployment without certificates to unemployment with certificates. While some might correctly see this as an inherent systemic problem of cap-italism, it is ideologised more often as a 'legacy of apartheid' and an indicator of the failure of the youth to take opportunities post-apartheid.

Despite the positive claims made by the minister, there are now at least three waves of youth who have failed, by official accounts, to meet the model required of them by the new South Africa: the *marginalised* youth of the 1980s, the *entitled* youth who followed and sometimes included them, and the *apathetic* youth of the new millennium. Each of them is portrayed as failing to make a productive contribution to economic growth—understood as capitalist profitability and competitiveness in the global economy. Against this measure, despite increasing opportunities for which youth are not increasingly grateful, the problem of lack of skills and unemployability runs through. Rising above these failures—as the role models representing what the new South Africa was always meant to be about in this ideologised *ex post facto* vision—are the successful black business entrepreneurs and functionaries of the capitalist state bureaucracy. These are the dream teams of the private and commercialised public sectors, sometimes in public-private partnership, sometimes extended into corporatist partnership between capital and labour at the workplace. Just as the political contributions of today's and tomorrow's youth are being constructed as socially valuable or not, relative to their places in the hierarchy of the market, so the contribution of the youth of the past is being reconstructed as part of a unilinear progression to greater or lesser achievement on the ladder of business success.

In this paper I try to outline another way of seeing the youth. While accepting that many youth were not and are not now involved in political activism, my concern is to identify what might be called a particular youth culture in an ongoing history of youth activism, running across waves of what have been dismissed as failures. In the main part of the paper, I first sketch some of the main features of the political context out of which youth activism grew and which it in turn helped to shape and develop. I then look at two examples of youth activism from the 1980s and early 1990s (the last years of the apartheid regime), drawn from different political traditions. These are snapshots into the lives which helped create the youth activism and shape the broader struggle of which it was part. I believe that the youth involved brought with them and developed a culture which was inherently oppositional and subversive towards the individualist and competitive values of the market, a vision of a different future of sharing and collectivism so that change should embrace all, and a willingness to sacrifice in pursuit of that vision. While these were features of the general mass movement of struggle and working-class struggle in particular, the youth also brought with them the added dimensions of an impatient insistence that change should happen in the lived experience of the here and now, and a particular energy in their willingness to sacrifice themselves in pursuit of that change.

The context

In 1973 a wave of strikes of non-unionised and largely unskilled workers heralded the resurgence of struggle. In 1976, youth in their millions across the country rose in direct confrontation, first with the educational authorities, then with the police, then with state structures in general. In 1979, after surviving a range of attacks from employers and the government, the survival of trade union organisation was reflected in the formation of the Federation of SA Trade Unions (Fosatu), followed by the Council of Unions of South Africa (CUSA) in 1980. Fosatu joined with some independent unions and CUSA's National Union of Mineworkers to form the Congress of South African Trade Unions (Cosatu) in 1984.[4] Youth, women's and civic organisation was developed across the country, usually out of direct mobilisation and confrontation. Particularly after 1981, partly in direct response to growing opposition inside the country from which it had sometimes been distant, the Congress Alliance through the ANC military wing mKhonto weSizwe (MK) embarked on more visible sabotage tactics. On the basis of an existing tradition, this won it increasing popularity amongst workers and youth directly facing the repressive force of the state. A number of youth who had left the country in 1976 returned from exile with military training, weapons and targets. The South African Congress of Youth (Sayco) was formed during the state of emergency of 1985. Many youth in schools prioritised the boycott as a weapon, rallying behind the slogan *Liberation before education*. While the slogan was and is debated as a guide to action, it reflected the impatience and willingness to sacrifice of a layer of youth for whom the struggle had been chosen and become the first and the immediate priority.[5] Sayco's slogan *Victory or death, victory is certain*—reflects the same features of the political culture of a militant, mobilised youth.

In 1986 there was a sharp increase in strike activity and in 1987 the largest strike wave in South African history. This was followed in 1988 by the biggest ever stay-away. Increasingly the main broad organisation of resistance, the United Democratic Front (UDF), and the strongest trade union formation, Cosatu, expressed their support for the ANC. There was a mounting recognition, even amongst elements within the ruling class, that a growing, mobilised and increasingly determined movement of resistance was rendering apartheid unsustainable as a system of government and control. At the same time, workers and youth in struggle searched for the politics and forms of mobilisation with which they could defend themselves and move forward.

In this context, it was not difficult for a socialist politics and vision which asserted the primacy of the working class to connect with workers and youth activists. In fact, no politics was going to connect if it was not grounded in what they knew and could recognise as most oppressive and most liberating in their lives. Nor was it difficult, in promoting socialist ideas, to ground them in recognition of and respect for the strength of organised and mobilised workers. The 1987 strike upsurge involved more than half the workers in Cosatu, many of the strikes being illegal. More than three million workers, including large numbers of non-unionised workers, joined the 1988 stay-away, also illegal. Millions of workers had rendered the apartheid Pass Laws of apartheid unenforceable by squatting illegally. It was *visibly* that strength which confronted employers, the government and the system—*and which survived and grew.* The experience of survival, struggle and successes, was shaping the vision of a different future.

Youth and workers

The youth of the 1980s developed politically in this context of mobilisation, confrontation and defiance when, to themselves, to each other, and to many others around them, workers, their organisations, and what they did and thought mattered. An orientation to the 'worker-student alliance' which was to guide millions in action and vision, no matter what their organisational political allegiances, was laid in the preparatory mobilisations for the historic Vaal stay-away in November 1984.[6] A pamphlet put out by the school students' organisation addressed workers:

Workers workers, build support for the students struggle in the schools…

Like you workers: we want democratic committees under our control (SRC's) to fight for our needs.

Like you workers: we students are prepared to fight all and every dismissal from our schools

Like you workers: we defend older students from being thrown out of schools, just like you defend old workers from being thrown out of factories

Like you workers: demand free overalls and boots so we students demand free books and schooling. And students don't pay for books and schools. IT IS THE WORKERS WHO PAY

Just as the workers: fight assaults against the workers in the factory, so we students fight against the beatings we get in school....

WORKERS YOU ARE FATHERS AND MOTHERS, YOU ARE OUR BROTHERS AND SISTERS. OUR STRUGGLE IN THE SCHOOLS IS YOUR STRUGGLE IN THE FACTORIES. WE FIGHT THE SAME BOSSES GOVERNMENT. WE FIGHT THE SAME ENEMY.

Today the bosses government has closed many of our schools. OUR BOY-COTT WEAPON IS NOT STRONG ENOUGH AGAINST OUR COMMON ENEMY, THE BOSSES AND THEIR GOVERNMENT...

WE STUDENTS WILL NEVER WIN OUR STRUGGLE WITHOUT THE STRENGTH AND SUPPORT FROM THE WORKERS MOVEMENT

Congress of SA Students Transvaal Region[7]

A T-shirt produced for the youth in 1984 by the metalworkers' union MAWU proclaimed: *Worker of the future*. Workers, their knowledge, what they did, their social weight, were all affirmed. There was pride and hope in being a worker. It was an identity to be respected—and aspired to for youth. Young workers and other activists searched memory, each other, history, the world, political texts, for ideas and knowledge, bringing everything into their intellectual embrace. The history of mass resistance, suppressed and stolen from popular memory, was rediscovered, re-appropriated, re-remembered by the millions who had made parts of it. Youth and other activists rescued, re-appropriated and reconstructed a history of militant struggle which had been suppressed and obscured.

There was a deeply *inclusive* spirit—the demands of the time ended with 'for all': decent housing for all; jobs for all; a living wage for all. A deeply-rooted tradition of participatory workers' democracy was growing. Partly as a statement of developments which had occurred, and partly as a statement of developments which had been made possible, *Cosatu News* argued that 'we need the same democracy tomorrow in our country that we are build-ing today in our movement...We are building democracy today in our struggles and in our organisations. Tomorrow we will build that mass-based democracy in our society.'[8] These and other features made up a subversive tradition—directly and explicitly politically challenging to both apartheid and the capitalist system which it protected.

While this phase of struggle has sometimes been characterised as 'only oppositional', the opposition was embodied in a set of experiences, practices, structures and—sometimes—policies. In the opposition was the embryonic alternative, workers and youth creating space within a brutal system and state of emergency in which they collectively controlled aspects of their own lives. There was a vision of the future based on the *alternatives* being created in the present, a future in which all of these things would be developed, so that the role which workers and youth played in shaping their own organisations extended into the workplace and the community and moulded a future in which this embryonic alternative dominated society. If such vision was necessarily oppositional, it also involved learning about building, developing, mobilising, thinking strategically, planning, innovating, improvising, encouraging, motivating, sharing, drawing out contributions from the widest possible layers of society. Increasingly, this necessarily totalising vision was called socialism. If the present did not belong to workers, the future would. The dominant banner of the National Union of Mineworkers claimed: *Socialism means freedom.* For some, the vision was sloganised in this way: *The youth are the workers of the future. The future belongs to the workers. The workers' future is a socialist future.* If youth turned to the organised strength of workers, workers acclaimed the militant mobilisations of youth. A message from the Executive Committee of Cosatu in 1987 argued:

> Our struggle has come a long way because of the determination of millions of people led by workers and youth…. Like our unions in the workplaces, street committees will give us the democratic organisation and unity and strength to fight for all the things we need—including control over every aspect of our lives through our own democratic organisation under the leadership of organised workers…the strongest, best and most reliable allies of the working class are the youth. Like us, the youth exploit no-one. They have nothing to lose and everything to gain by marching together with us to a workers' future. We are committed to the leadership of the working class in the struggle.'[9]

There was much debate and differing views about the 'leadership of the working class'. While there was clearly stated political insistence on working-class leadership inside the broader movement of struggle, as we have seen from Cosatu, what was the difference between the different formulations used such as 'worker leadership', 'the leading role of workers', 'a leading role', 'a leading force', 'the vanguard of the struggle', 'the leadership of the struggle'? What did working class leadership mean to those who did not accept a class analysis and did not accept that there was a class struggle, or that workers should be fighting it?

I am not going to go into those issues here, but even opponents of working-class leadership in the struggle found themselves forced to search for formulations which connected with the reality in the lived experience and in the minds of growing numbers of workers and youth. It was just not possible, in the prevailing political culture, to directly oppose the idea, and still strike a chord with the popular sentiment and experience. For growing numbers of workers and youth, the 'socialist orientation' and 'workers' interpretation' of the Freedom Charter, the 'leading role of the working-class' and 'working-class leadership', 'worker democracy' and 'worker control' and the 'nationalisation' of the future all coalesced. They embodied a vision which actually went far beyond, and in fact politically challenged, the formal and actual policy decisions of the ANC and its Congress Alliance allies even while they were often reflected in support for the Congress movement. With whatever uncertainties, they all meant a collectivist future without oppression or exploitation in which workers controlled their own lives and the wealth was used under worker control to meet human needs; a future where class power would be in the hands of the working class—under the increasingly popularised name of socialism.

It was in this highly politicised context of the mid and late 1980s that the youth activists who are explored in this paper grew up and developed politically. However complex, contradictory and changing, it was a context characterised also by hope, by the vision of a different and better future and by mass mobilisations infused with that vision.[10] Ernst Bloch said that 'to be human is really to have utopias',[11] that 'thinking means venturing beyond'.[12] Trotsky has written of the way in which revolution is characterised by ordinary workers 'interfering'. In the depths of apartheid oppression and the capitalist exploitation it protected, millions of ordinary workers survived, resisted, and started to imagine and shape the collective future. They ventured beyond, made themselves human, and started to make real what had not yet become. All of this was there to be seen, as collectives of workers and youth activists confronted the issues which faced them and acted together to make and change history.

Comrade Bongani

It has become a truism in the new South Africa that no-one ever supported apartheid. Equally it has also become common knowledge that no-one was ever struggling for the armed seizure of power and the appropriation of private property by the working class. Former functionaries of apartheid say: 'We thought we were fighting against a communist onslaught.' Erstwhile self-declared communists shake their heads in disbelief. Then the two former antagonists unite in looking for ways of promoting competitiveness and attracting foreign investment. But there were youth and workers who believed that the struggle could never be won without armed defence and resistance; there were revolutionary communists in South Africa; there was a period in the anti-apartheid struggle in which millions of workers and youth organised and mobilised in many forms of mass action behind policies and slogans which increasingly included support for socialism and working-class power. For most, this meant support for the South African Communist Party (SACP). Others found 'the Party' to be a major obstacle in pursuing their own communist beliefs. In what follows about the life and struggles of one such comrade, I draw on three main primary sources: my own contact and knowledge of the youth activist involved; comments and discussion about him from other comrades; and documents of the Trotskyist organisation whose policies and method he finally came to embrace.

Comrade Bongani was one of those whose socialist vision was a guide to action. His search for action, ideas, policies and programme which would advance the workers' revolution took him first into and then out of the SACP. Bongani was from Chiawelo, a part of the massive Soweto 'township'. At the time of the 1973 strikes, he was eight years old. Bongani heard stories of the struggle of the past from his father—a worker and lay preacher. His mother died when he was very young—he talked of a sister who was a domestic worker whom he used to visit at her place of work. As he grew up, friends became comrades. Talking involved listening, learning, sharing, questioning and challenging; they talked about many things, but more and more about 'the struggle.' Comrades were those who threw stones with him, gathered weapons, and survived attacks (or sometimes did not); they were those who looked for organisation and ideas which could take their revolutionary energy forward. Together in the streets, on mass mobilisations, at funerals, and in meetings they sang songs of youth and sacrifice:

Asinakubulawa
We youth
We'll never fall prey
To these whites.
We will never fall prey
To these whites.
We are so young.

So young
So young.

And:

We'll leave our parents
And go to exile
We'll fight for our land
South Africa.
Don't cry mother
Till death
I will fight for our country
South Africa.

Bongani was one of a small minority of 'African' township youth who went to university.[13] While he was studying at the University of the Witwatersrand, he helped develop the Workers' School out of a literacy project. This was an initiative to 'redeploy' some of the resources of the university to the advantage of the workers who were denied access—except to clean and to labour. Bongani arrived as a shy, quiet, almost withdrawn volunteer. Over time, he became the director of the school and later was employed by one of the country's leading progressive educational institutions, Khanya. In 1991, Bongani published in the newsletter of the Workers' School a poem written by his comrade Trevor Ngwane. It captured their shared thinking.

Who are you? They asked me
Who am I? I replied
I am a worker
My job is to make revolution
I am a fighter
My war is
Against exploitation
I am student
My field is human history
I am a Marxist
My cause is socialism
I am a poet
My poem is
Liberation
I am a singer

My song is Fridom [*sic*]
I am a prophet
My prophecy is
Communism
I am a dreamer
My dream is
Human equality
I am a writer
My book is class struggle
I am a swimmer
My water is the masses
I am a guerrilla
My gun is
Mass action
I am a lion
My roar is revolution
I am a Messiah
My heaven is society without classes
I am God Almighty
My command is
Be ready to die for the struggle.[14]

Bongani started to see in the working class and the independent class politics of Marxism the only alternative to capitalist class rule and the only hope for the socialist revolution. This led him into consistent strike support activities from the university. Contact with railway workers in the 1987 strikes brought many of them into the Workers' School. Before the unbanning of organisations in 1990, Bongani was leader of his street and block committee working at the grassroots in addressing residents' problems and mobilising against apartheid policies. One of the big campaigns at the time was the rent boycott and Bongani was at the forefront of numerous meetings and activities building this. Despite mythologies about South Africa's 'peaceful transition', workers and youth militants faced physical attacks from a range of official and unofficial state structures. While chairperson of an ANC branch and then secretary of an SACP branch, both in Soweto, he played an active role in acquiring weapons legally where possible, illegally where necessary. He was elected the organiser of the defence squad—a situation which placed him in conflict with ANC politics which located armed defence and resistance in the hands of MK alone. As Ngwane puts it:

Bongani's line was 'Build self-defence units, build the workers' militia!' The work of defence was politically linked to the dream of socialism and a society where every worker would be armed in defence of the revolution and where there would be no professional army but workers themselves.[15]

As eyes turned to the prospect of elections in the early 1990s, he demanded of the freedom of the future what has proved so far to be 'unrealistic'. As he put it: 'The vote must bring porridge into the pot.'[16] In Bongani's everyday life—as in the life of many youth and worker activists about whom papers are not written—the words of poems and pamphlets and political slogans guided his action. They were continually tested in the heat of struggle. They led him to search for the strongest possible forms of organisation and action—in the boycotts, on the streets, on picket lines, in the various mass organisations, in worker education activities, in mobilising strike support, building self-defence units—in seeking always for the most developed and advanced theoretical understanding and programme. He did not desert them, as some have done. Like many facing the daily realities of struggle at the time, he believed that the struggle could not be won peacefully. Over the Easter week-end of 1994, having survived one earlier attempted assassination, he was shot and found dead several hours later in the street, apparently dumped from a moving car. He was 26. Everyone who knew him believes this was a political assassination. We also believed and believe that his killers will never be tried and convicted.

To those who knew him and loved him, worked with him, were his comrades, trusted him with their lives, Bongani was special. Some might say that his assassination marked him out, or that the elected leadership positions he held indicated that he was special. But many people have paid with their lives, in obvious and less obvious ways, for South Africa's 'peaceful transition'. I think he would have been the first to deny that holding elected positions made him special. And I think that, in the core of this denial, something special which Bongani represented can be illuminated. It could be called respect for the working class, involving recognition of what Gramsci has called the organic capacity of the working class, what Rosa Luxemburg affirmed as spontaneity, what Trotsky respected as interference, what led Lenin to argue that strikes were schools of war which promoted an instinctive move towards socialist politics. A pamphlet distributed by Bongani put it in this way:

Give people the chance to act together—and they produce strength and ideas and wealth that no-one believed was possible. Look at the old man who has been bent down quiet at work for a starvation wage for thirty years. Listen to the knowledge that he has got to share, when he can lift up his head during a strike. Look at the old woman who has spent her life looking after the children of the rich madam, while her own children were hungry. She is the one who can remind us when our spirits are low: 'We must continue in this struggle. It is not only for us today. It is for our children also tomorrow'…Mass action is a school where we learn together. It is a school where we get the chance to share our knowledge. It is a school where everyone is a learner and everyone is a teacher. In that school, we are already creating the future.[17]

It was in this political culture that Bongani became who he was. Its key features were exactly what he would most want to have talked about, celebrated and focused our attention on. They are about what he believed—and what he believed is what he did. They allowed him as a youth activist to embrace and build his socialist vision in the heat of a mobilised working-class struggle; to look up and see the future, to see in every situation of working class life the seeds of what could be, not just what was. This visionary political culture invited him to share, and emboldened him to dream.

In 1990, a leader of the SACP claimed the support of '90% of COSATU and the youth'.[18] Like many activists Bongani originally joined the SACP because he was searching for a revolutionary politics beyond the class collaboration demanded by reformist politics then dominating the ANC. He found, however, that as a member of the SACP he was expected to defend class collaboration against militants seeking to challenge it inside the ANC and other organisations. During the negotiations between the government and the ANC, Bongani had to make sense of a situation in which the ANC/SACP leadership was warning against the mass action that he celebrated. He had to work out how it could be that the capitalists he had learned to hate were increasingly being embraced as 'social partners' and 'compatriots'. He came to the answer that the politics of class collaboration could only serve those same capitalists and their system. Finally, like many militants of that time, he could not make sense of the party's role as advocate of 'sunset' clauses.[19] It became impossible for him to pursue his socialist politics while advocating the constitutional protection of private property. This was a dilemma many faced. After taking up the issue extensively in his SACP branch, he put commitment to a politics and class before loyalty to an organisation and resigned. This was not an easy thing to do. It laid him open to accusations of disloyalty to 'the struggle'. It also meant leaving behind comrades with whom he had stood and fought in that struggle. While he found an organisational home inside the Workers' League, a grouping based on the political tradition of Marx, Lenin and Trotsky, he had to leave behind the authority of 'the Party'. All he had now in the struggle was his energy and vision, his politics, his comrades, and the workers. But that is also where he had started, and how he had moved forward, and what made him who he was.

The story of Bongani represents a specific form of the culture of political activism amongst youth. Given Bongani's politics, it was characterised by a particularly consciously developed respect for the working class, in addition to features of sacrifice, impatience and militancy characteristic amongst the youth more generally. This was a minority position and it could be argued that visionary youth activists like Bongani have been cast into the shadows of 'official history' exactly because they were a minority and hostile to key aspects of the dominant political positions of the ANC/SACP leaderships. But such was the social weight of the working class and the strength of the working class in the day to day dynamics of political struggle that it commanded respect—even from layers of youth in political traditions which did not necessarily foreground or even acknowledge that. It promoted a vision of a post-apartheid future, increasingly called by the name 'socialism' whose influence went far beyond political minorities and deep into the ranks of youth vigorously loyal to the ANC/SACP. Grounded in the visible strength of mobilised workers, imbued by the impatience and militancy of youth, this vision was in effect in conflict with the formal stages theory of revolution in official SACP policy.

One such grouping of youth was represented in the Bonteheuwel Military Wing (BMW), firmly within the political tradition of the Congress Alliance, strongly influenced by some prominent individual leaders of the ANC and SACP. In the next part of this paper, I turn to aspects of their history. If Bongani is remembered by those who knew and worked with him, many of the former militants of the BMW are there to remember their own history. In proceeding to look at BMW, we are looking not only at a reconstruction of history, but also at the recall and memory of those who made it. In what follows, I draw on interviews conducted by Salma Ismail, formerly a teacher at Bonteheuwel High, public texts, and direct contact with some of the youth involved. The interviews were conducted in May and July 1997 and January 1998. The interviews were transcribed but the transcriptions are not publicly available and identities are not revealed without the agreement of the individuals concerned, or unless public records are used.[20]

Bonteheuwel Military Wing

The Vaal stay-away of 1984 represented a coming together of student boycotts and community and worker mobilisation. By 1985, boycotts had become ordinary across the country. There were few black schools in which formal education proceeded 'as normal'. Bonteheuwel is a particularly impoverished working-class suburb in greater Cape Town. In apartheid terms, it was a 'Coloured' area. The youth of BMW grew up in the same broader political context as Bongani, but there were specificities. As the elections in 1994 indicated, Bonteheuwel was in fact a stronghold of electoral support for apartheid's National Party. Unlike the situation in much of the country, the activist youth of Bonteheuwel generally had to face the forces of the state without the immediate physical and political, support, protection and sometimes discipline of the mass of mobilised workers. They drew sympathy and were given hiding by a layer of family and community supporters, but, on the streets in direct confrontation, the youth were largely on their own. Nonetheless, an activist core made the youth of Bonteheuwel a major national force in direct action against the state and in promoting the schools boycott behind the slogan: 'Liberation before education.' As with many activists, they used the local schools, even while boycotted, as centres for organisation, agitation and mobilisation. Initially youth in Bonteheuwel schools were organised in the Bonteheuwel Inter School Congress, (Bisco) part of the regional affiliate of Sayco. A special action group was set up to promote 'ungovernability'—in line with ANC calls. They were known as the Bisco military wing. Over time, this action group separated itself from broader control of more cautious and less militant elements and started calling themselves Bonteheuwel Military Wing.

Activities such as awareness / alternative education programmes, placard demonstrations, marches, rallies, street action (stonings, petrol bomb attacks and burning barricades), meetings, stay-aways, funerals, court cases dominated the day. These were met by the most brutal force of the police and army who routinely whipped students, parents and teachers, tear-gassed them, sprayed bird-shot, rubber bullets and later live ammunition into crowds of people. Under the State of Emergency the police and security forces detained people without trial for 14 days; others were held in solitary confinement for 90 days; many of the youth were tortured in jail and suffered severe physical and psychological abuse. In 1986, the BMW came under the command of MK, although exact lines of command and accountability remain an issue of some dispute and uncertainty. A few BMW activists received military training outside South Africa but most were trained internally.

At leadership levels, the youth were given particular responsibility for deepening the campaign of 'ungovernability'. This meant, on the one hand, continuing and often indiscriminate harassment, intimidation and violence from state forces, and on the other, the further development of a widespread and deep-rooted willingness to endanger and sacrifice self for the broader 'struggle'. Revolutionary status and becoming both an identified opponent and target of the police afforded militants a glamour and broader community recognition which ordinary life could not provide.

T describes his understanding of the word at the time:

> The struggle was like religion, the more you learn about it, the more addictive you become and crazy, because you do it with your heart you become a slave of the struggle and think that you will achieve freedom if you spill your blood. Although you are making many sacrifices for your family and community you become blinded and can't see that they are hurt when you have no time for them.

Another former activist, *M*, says:

> Those were the best times of my life, there was something to live for, to die for, there was honour, true comradeship, strangers were prepared to accept you into their house and look out for you, they would give you a place to sleep and a plate of food, they saw you fighting for things that they could not fight for.

After years of frenzied activity both inside and outside the schools the leadership of the BMW were under death threats from the police and other security forces. Special units within the security forces had been assigned to 'eliminate' key leaders.[21] This situation forced three of the most respected leaders to go into exile . Two of them were killed within a few months of their return and two further leading activists were assassinated during a military operation. These events had dramatic effects on the BMW who were already facing more and more other pressures. They had developed with a dependence on particular individual leaders and when these people were either forced into exile or murdered, they were left disorientated, and with deepening internal distrust and tensions. In this context, with community support uneven and sometimes wavering, police attack and intimidation continuing, demoralisation, political uncertainty, and vulnerability to state informers began to mount. The response of the existing leadership tended to be to insist on discipline and militancy, without fully addressing the factors which were undermining these and revealing their limitations.

BMW had developed and been developed as the foot-soldiers of 'ungovernability'. Their development was characterised, *inter alia*, by clandestine existence, the dictates of survival under constant state repression, uneasy relationships with other organisations within the broader liberation movement and their tradition of particularly charismatic and powerful individual leaders. In the later part of 1987 and 1988 they had to face increasingly visible moves by the Congress Alliance into negotiations with the apartheid regime. In a fundamental sense, the foot-soldiers of 'ungovernability' were being rendered redundant by processes in which their own militancy had no respect nor stable place. While a core of members of BMW had developed the skills necessary for more efficient and organised confrontations with the forces of the state, their training left them without adequate preparation and ill-equipped to deal with the mounting pressures of political direction, relations with other parts of the community and the climate of mistrust which the state had fostered. Other members of BMW were not prepared for the viciousness and persistence of state repression. All of these factors created conditions which made the continued survival of BMW increasingly difficult and at the same time, allowed openings which the forces of the state exploited.

Remembering the struggle

BMW members had to decide how to relate to the Truth and Reconciliation Commission (TRC), tasked with documenting gross violations of human rights in the apartheid era. On the surface, as with many other people who contributed in different ways to the struggle, this should have been an opportunity for them to tell their story, have their role recognised and receive some form of compensation for their contribution and sacrifices. The reality has proved less 'romantic' than that. Essentially, the TRC assigned to youth activists the identity of 'victims' or 'perpetrators'. Some went to the TRC to talk of their pride as survivors and soldiers in their collective contribution to the struggle, only to find that the TRC dealt with them as individual victims. Others chose silence, rather than 'confessing' to what in TRC terms classifies them as 'perpetrators'.[22]

Sandra Adonis joined the struggle when she was 15, moving from house to house in the townships, helping make bullets and firebombs. She says she lost her youth, education and a stable home. The 'struggle' changed her husband into a violent, angry man. He has since died. She was unemployed and wanted the commission to help her start a new life but feels that she has got nothing. 'I feel like many other victims who came to the TRC to end the nightmare, to tell of the pain but feel that the perpetrators of human abuses seem to be getting far more out of the commission than those who were brutalised'. She says that if she had the choice again, she would never have testified about her life as a guerrilla.[23]

Like others, she struggles to assert a pride in her role:

Although we have done things that we are not proud of but the reasons why we have done it we are proud of them, because today we can stand with our heads up high and say that we are together with the nation, we have done it!

Just like the Boers who have been interrogating us and torturing us, they are trying to say to us today we are sorry we did not mean that. But I say we do not need their apologies, well, I certainly do not need them because I think my life is messed up as it is, directionless. I lost my education, my childhood and my youth. Although we have received our freedom, our democracy but we in BMW gave, we have not gained anything, we are still unemployed, homeless, abandoned. In fact this time at these hearings is the first time that people have shown an interest in us.[24]

Faried Verhaelst says he believes that the commission has let many people down; he did not find the act of giving public testimony comforting. Verhaelst was a BMW member who was tortured for weeks by the South African security police. He said they tried new methods each night, from beatings to electric shocks, to hanging, to putting a gun up his rectum. 'I had started to put it away and sleep at night. But after the hearings I couldn't put my head on a pillow again'.[25] Verhaelst in his testimony to the TRC said that he was not just speaking for himself but the other comrades that had to be taken care of. It hurt that they had sacrificed their lives for the struggle and now nobody is looking after them. Some have jobs but do not know how to keep them; others are still full of hatred and vengeance and cannot deal with these emotions. For *T* the TRC was wrong:

[I]t's a slap in the face walking over the dignity of our fallen heroes. We went into the struggle to die for our people, you can't claim money for holding such beliefs or someone's contribution to the struggle, they decided to go into the struggle, they knew the price, they are martyrs of the cause. The worst thing someone can do to me is to go to the TRC and ask for money for me as this does not bring back commitment; rather let them tell our children what we did, what the struggle meant to us. We want them to know the bitterness, the loneliness, and sweat as well as the heroic parts. This will also bring truth and healing.

A study of the testimony of youth at the TRC has characterised them as 'between anger and hope'.[26] Interviews and other data reveal a picture of BMW members deeply disillusioned by the current situation. They speak of betrayal in many different voices and have been unable to recover from the dual shock of police brutality and of feeling abandoned by the ANC government. One member put it in this way to the TRC:

> Apartheid scarred me for most of my life—firstly there was repression, poverty, racism, growing up in a township with little prospects of escaping my fate of unemployment, gangsterism, drugs, alcohol—for these reasons I saw in the 'struggle' a way to the future therefore went into political activism and because of these actions endured detentions, torture, trauma and now I end up psychologically scarred, with no education, no skills and unemployable—my fate seems unchanged whether I had joined the struggle or not.[27]

As has been shown, this is a view which is accompanied at times by expressions of great pride. There are no doubt other views. But what is encountered and documented is a *real* view and it is given weight each day by the reality of the situation in which many BMW and other activists find themselves. In circumstances of material hardship with little immediate hope, pride tends to be submerged. The testimony of former BMW activists is permeated with their alienation from the vision and hope which drove them. This involves an apparent distance between aspects of the history as they were seen at the time, and the reconstruction of that history by the people who made it at the time. The sense of sacrifice is there, but the hope and the impatience and the vision are partly lost in apparent disillusion. One aspect of the culture—the willingness to sacrifice, is set up in tension against other aspects—the vision of a future that would be better and different, that would extend to all, that would be won in the here and now, not shifted to some increasingly remote 'stage' of the future. It is unfortunately not difficult to explain this tension. The reality is too often that, at best, for the youth activists under discussion, nothing tangible has come out of the willingness to sacrifice behind the demand for real change now. It is a reality replicated in the daily lives of millions of people, and millions more for whom whatever has changed had not addressed the poverty of everyday life. At worst, that willingness is itself being denigrated in favour of the contextually dominant value of individual competitiveness. It is a value which comes into direct conflict with any developed respect for the working class as collective—and for collectivist vision and politics. If that was the case when the social weight of the working class was so dominant in struggle, it is even more so in the more recent context which has been characterised by the rising social weight of the black middle class and an expanding layer of black capitalists.

Sense of loss

The many, many stories and accounts of hopes and fears and achievements and dreams create an overwhelming sense of loss. Former activists use many different words and sometimes choose specific silences to convey a sense that they have lost their youth, their role, their pride, their achievements, affirmation for their strengths and qualities and contribution, their vision of what the future under liberation would mean, their history; and with that goes another loss, the loss of their opportunities in life. At times they confront a new, officially sanctioned and stabilised notion of history, in which youth such as the soldiers of BMW are being relegated to the shadows as incidental stone-throwers. There is increasing distancing, often largely retrospective, from the impatient, militant slogans and approach which characterised their struggle and behind which they were willing to mobilise and sacrifice. Supposed limitations of 'emotional', 'unrealistic', and 'outdated' slogans and demands are announced and ridiculed in the new climate of the struggle for international competitiveness. The harsh irony is that history has developed in a way which actually conforms to their slogans: their liberation did actually come before their (formal certificated) education. Great numbers of youth who mobilised behind slogans like Victory or death and actually did offer their lives to the struggle are, in official history, being dismissed as a generation who expected something for nothing—representatives of the 'culture of entitlement'. Alternatively, they are allowed by the TRC to be either perpetrators or victims. If their slogans embodied the bravado of youth, they also reflected the reality of millions who, on a practical day to day level, were willing to run risks and sacrifice even their lives. There is nothing about a culture of 'hand-outs' in any of that. There is insistence that sacrifice should bring results and a deep-rooted impatience in achieving those results. That is neither the stuff of victims nor perpetrators, but of rank and file soldiers in a struggle for real change. And there is something about entitlement in that. Not in the sense that it has come to be so easily and constructed and dismissed, as 'something for nothing', but in the much deeper sense of a vision of what change should mean: a social reality in which ordinary people would have as their rights, that to which they were entitled above anything else: real safety and security and comfort for all, lives allowed to be the best they can be, filled with humaneness, solidarity and happiness.

The core of Bongani's life was organisation and action driven by socialist vision and hope in the socialist future. The message of his life is that such hope lives when it is grounded in the capacity of workers to collectively organise and mobilise in their own interests. In conditions which struggle has made so much easier in many ways, Marxists and the broader left are having to learn how to survive and build without the immediate receptivity of a mobilised workers' movement. It is easy, in that context, to blame workers, to resort to nostalgia, or to surrender in the name of 'realism'. All of that would have been easy also in the 1960s when things were not moving forward. But workers interfered, and created a new and different history, increasingly looking up and seeing the only possible future other than barbarism.

Bongani grew up and developed as a youth activist in a context dominated by the political strength of a mobilised workers' movement. He came to develop a politics which consciously recognised that fact and embraced a vision of socialism which rested upon the role of the working class. The activists of BMW grew up and developed politically in the same context. But, even in the height of working class mobilisations, there was a political separation between their guerrillaist activism and the day to day development of that mobilisation. To the extent that there was a conscious socialist vision, it was often *on behalf of* the working class, not by and of and in support of the working class. This made them more vulnerable to an alienation when they had to look for ways of sustaining their own militancy outside of that context—in a period of ebb and demobilisation. If their own confrontations with the state had become the centres of their political universe, they were all also emboldened to dream and encouraged—given courage—to engage with the state, and sometimes in fact protected by mass working class mobilisation in the broader context around them. Taking guidance and sometimes orders from ANC and SACP ideologues who did not recognise this, lacking political and logistical support, they were left stranded. Their impatience, militancy, courageous energy and willingness to sacrifice had been enough in one context to motivate them and sustain their vision; for many, it was not enough in the new context.

Neither Bongani nor the activists of the BMW would have been in the struggle and stayed there without hope.[28] That hope is now part of history. More often, it is an obscured and denied part of history. But what of memories of hope, memories of hope as hope, renewals of hope? Pumzile Gobodo-Mdikizela has commented on the way in which trauma can so easily become part of collective memory.[29] The other side of the coin is the difficulty for hope and for a collectivist vision which was a crucial driving force of history to be given their place in a context where they are neither currently experienced or affirmed. But if hope and collectivism, and the hope of collectivism grounded on respect for the working class, are no longer affirmed but in fact denigrated, this does not mean that they were not realities in the situation—possibilities created in struggle.

An early worker booklet of the period was entitled *The sun shall rise for the workers*.[30] Increasingly that future was called by the name of socialism—however that was understood. 'It is a future so different to the hardship and suffering of today that sometimes, it is hard even to imagine it.'[31] But it was imagined. Imagining that future, as with Bloch's 'thinking', means venturing beyond, developing a vision of possibilities which have not yet become. This involves recognition of the seeds in the present of a different future, of negation and transformation. It is a deeply revolutionary and hopeful vision. There is another, dominant social vision of youth based on what they 'are not' and what they 'are not yet'. In this view, youth are not yet adult, not yet mature, not yet really people. They are in the process of becoming—at an early step on a unilinear path which is predetermined and whose historical destination is 'success'. Success as entrepreneur, success as wealth, success in competition, success as individual. It is an overwhelmingly dominant view and lies at the root of all dismissals of youth as failures, unless they 'make it' in a social context in which structurally, making it for one is predicated on not making it for hundreds. It is analytically reinforced by the reduction of youth to a sociologised category in which they are characterised predominantly as the social carriers and repository of problems: youth gangsterism, youth pregnancy, youth HIV, youth unemployment, youth apathy. Outside of this, they can, at best, be miniature versions of success—'youth entrepreneur', and/or consumers—the 'youth market'.

Against this view is the hope of recognising in youth a different and better possibility for the future; it is based on a celebration of the fact that they have not yet become, exactly because they carry with them the seeds of becoming something better and different—better in large part because it is different. In this view, what is dismissed as a culture of entitlement becomes celebrated as a passion for what human beings need and can collectively provide for each other. What is dismissed as the impatience of youth as part of that same culture of entitlement becomes celebrated as an insistence that something better and different should be made part of their present—that change and the different future should happen now.

I have written this article conscious of the task of recording and affirming what is faced with so many powerful forms of dismissal and 'denialism'. But memory is not made or rescued or recalled by writing papers. I remember vividly how, at the height of the mobilisations of the 1980s, youth activists would search experience, history, resources centres, each other and the people around them for memories of former struggles. They would appropriate, as memory, what they had never experienced, making it part of who they were in their activist present. It is in the ongoing and renewed and emerging struggles that the memories currently suppressed and denied will again become parts of popular memory. Perhaps more than anywhere else, this process of renewal can currently be seen in what have been called the 'new social movements'. The youth are, again, the 'foot soldiers' of renewed political action. They still have the questions in front of them as those who went before: How do they relate to the working class? What part does 'totalising vision' play in their development? How do they deal with questions of power to create a qualitatively and fundamentally different and better world? Social movements—old, new or renewed, do not by their existence answer questions and make choices about class politics and the road to socialism and communism. By their continuity, emergence or renewal, they pose the reality of those questions and choices in everyday life. As they face these political tasks, I can see in the youth of the new social movements that same impatience and willingness to sacrifice which will be and are fundamental to new waves of struggle. More than anyone else, it is the youth who can renew a continuity of precisely these qualities; qualities which nurtured and promoted the traditions of struggle of a past which they can only hear about because they were not there. And those qualities will in turn infuse memory, shape and construct it to recapture and illuminate features which have been cast into shadow and discarded.

At the funerals of Bongani, murdered BMW cadres, and other activists, people pledged to 'pick up their spears.' Tebogo is now a couple of years younger than Bongani when he died. She is an activist of the Soweto Electricity Crisis Committee and Operation Khanyisa. She spends much of her time in mass mobilisations to struggle against water and electricity cut-offs imposed by ANC councils against defaulters. She recently heard about comrade Bongani and I asked her to write what she thought of his memory and youth apathy:

> The youth today, when their neighbours are being evicted for not paying services the first thing they say is: 'It serves him right, why they are not paying?' I don't think that is what comrade Bongani would say to a worker who's been evicted or retrenched
> The way people are living pains me because I know we can change it and it makes me sick to hear young people thinking like bosses…we need to change things for the next generation to come.
> To comrade Bongani: Comrade Bongani.
> You knew why we needed to fight against the oppressors
> You were a person with courage…with a vision to see socialism.
> They thought when they kill you
> There won't be someone to follow your steps…
> They thought the struggle would be over,
> But they didn't not know that there are people who will follow you.
> People who will follow your steps, people of your age.[32]

Key, visionary features of the culture of activism of many youth in the late 1980s are largely written out of official history with its 'stabilising mission'. It is part of the grander scheme of reshaping a future in which visions of the socialist future held in the past can not and will not be guides to action and a better changed society. Memory of collective hope and hope in collectivism are being lost in that revision. They are also being lost in a lived reality which does not sustain them. But ordinary people, in continuing, new, renewed or resurgent struggle, create renewed collectivism, as they create their own hope. Memory of hope can be memory as hope. And people with hope are emboldened to do and achieve things that people without hope have been forced to accept as impossible.

Notes

1. C. Hooper-Box, 'Nine million reasons to pay attention to the kwaito nation', *Sunday Independent*, 28 December 2003.
2. J. Grossman, 'The right to strike and worker freedom in and beyond apartheid', in T. Bass and M. van der Linden (eds.), *Free and Unfree Labour. The debate continues* (Bern, 1997), pp.145–70.
3. Quoted on the SAFM 7pm radio news broadcast, SABC, 30 December 2003.
4. J. Grossman, *For Our Children Tomorrow: Workers in Struggle in South Africa: 1973–1995* (Amsterdam, 1996); LACOM, *Freedom from Below* (Braamfontein, Johannesburg, undated); G. Kraak, *Breaking the Chains* (London, 1993), J. Baskin, *Striking Back* (Johannesburg, 1991).
5. S. Ismail and J. Grossman, '"Liberation now! education later!" Militants of the former Bonteheuwel Military Wing reflect on aspects of their struggle', *Education as Change*, 2 (2) (Johannesburg, 1998), pp.19–31; R. Jordi, 'Towards people's education—the boycott experience in Cape Town's Department of Education and Culture High Schools from July 1985 to February 1986', Honours dissertation, Faculty of Education, University of Cape Town (1987); M. Vassen, '"Beyond the barricades". The 1985 schools boycott and the vicissitudes of the Athlone Student Action Committee', Honours thesis, Faculty of Education, University of Cape Town (1995).
6. 'Student' was fluidly and loosely defined. It usually referred to youth of high school-going age. When primary school students joined mobilisations, they were often included in the category 'student'. It could also mean those in tertiary education. The youth focused on in this paper were generally between the ages of 13 and 25 at the time of events under discussion.
7. Labour Monitoring Group, 'The November stay-away', *South African Labour Bulletin*, 10 (6) (1985), pp.74–100.
8. Cosatu, 'Freedom Charter', *Cosatu News*, February 1989.
9. Cosatu, 'Message from the Cosatu Executive Committee to all members' (Mimeo, 1987).

10. J. Grossman, 'Working class collectivism: a legacy of hope for the new millennium?', *Proc. 11th International Oral History Conference, Istanbul, June 2000*, pp.788–94.

11. Quoted in R.H. Roberts, *Hope and its Hieroglyph* (Atlanta, 1990), p.29.

12. Quoted in R. Aronson, 'Hope after hope?', *Social Research*, 66 (2) (1999), p.472.

13. The terminology is not my own. It designates those who, under apartheid, would have been subject to the Pass Laws. After a period in the struggle in which different apartheid categories were rejected in favour of the unifying 'black', the categories are returning in the official and everyday use of many.

14. Wits Workers School, *Sunrise* (Johannesburg, undated, circa 1991).

15. T. Ngwane, personal correspondence (2004).

16. Quoted in T. Ngwane, 'He was a lion. A tribute to Comrade Bongani', document in my possession (1994).

17. Workers League, 'On Mass Action', document in my possession (Johannesburg, 1991).

18. M. Mayekiso, (interviewed by A. Callinicos), in A. Callinicos (ed.), *Between Apartheid and Capitalism* (London, 1990), p.112.

19. These were 'compromises' with the state and capitalist class, deemed by the ANC leadership to be necessary to ensure a transition without resistance from within the apartheid state and business. Key examples are the constitutional protection of private property, and guarantees to apartheid state employees.

20. I would like to thank Salma Ismail and the people interviewed. See also Truth and Reconciliation Commission, 1997, Youth hearings, 22 May, Hewat Colleage and 5–8 August, University of the Western Cape.

21. See Z. Khoisan, *Jakaranda Time. An investigator's view of South Africa's Truth and Reconciliation Commission* (Cape Town, 2001).

22. J. Grossman, 'Violence and silence: rewriting the future in South Africa', *Proc. 10th International Oral History Conference, Rio de Janeiro, 1999*, pp.1427–36. Also published as J. Grossman, 'Violencia y silencio: Reescribir el futuro. Silenciar la experiencia' la resistencia y la esperanza de la clase trabajadora', *Historia, Antropologia y Fuentes Orales*, 21 (Barcelona, 1999), pp.131–48.

23. S. Daley, 'In apartheid inquiry, agony is relived but not put to rest', *New York Times*, 17 July 1997.

24. TRC, Youth hearings.

25. Daley, 'In apartheid inquiry'.

26. K. Chubb and L. van Dijk, *Between Anger and Hope* (Johannesburg, 2001).

27. Y. Henry, 'Testimony to the TRC' (Mimeo, May 1997).

28. Grossman, 'Working class collectivism'.

29. *Mail and Guardian*, 11 July 2003.

30. M. Makhoba, *The Sun shall Rise for the Workers* (Braamfontein, Johannesburg, 1984).

31. Workers League, 'May Day', document in my possession (Johannesburg, 1984).

32. T. Mashota, personal correspondence (2004).

Tributes

Noreen Branson (1910–2003)

Noreen Branson, who died late last year at the age of 93, was for many years a highly valued and active member of the Socialist History Society and its predecessor, the Communist Party History Group. I knew her in later life, when she was a familiar face at meetings of the Society in London. She seemed essentially to be a very private person.

From early adulthood onwards she devoted her considerable talents and energies to the labour and socialist movement and the fight against poverty. In the early 1930s she joined the ILP, but soon transferred her allegiance to the Communist Party. Her aristocratic background proved invaluable cover for her missions as a Comintern courier in the 1930s, delivering money and documents to illegal communist parties in Europe and India. From 1938 until her death she was closely associated with the Labour Research Department. She edited *Labour Research* for almost 30 years, and developed a formidable expertise, among other things, on welfare and social security issues.

As a historian, Noreen's specialisms were 20th century British society and politics. She wrote several major books, including *Britain in the Nineteen Thirties* (with Margot Heinemann, 1971), *Britain in the Nineteen Twenties* (1975), *Popularism 1919–1925* (1979), and two volumes in Lawrence and Wishart's *History of the Communist Party of Great Britain* series (1985 and 1997). She was also the author of numerous articles, pamphlets and reviews.

Noreen wrote or contributed to several CP History Group and Socialist History Society publications, including *London Squatters 1946* (1989), and the *History of Labour-Communist Relations* (with Bill Moore, 1990 and 1991). She served on the CPHG and SHS committee for over twenty years, and was an editorial adviser to *Socialist History* from 1994 until her death. Her experience, wisdom and historical knowledge were a great asset to the society, as well as to the wider movement, and she will be sorely missed.

Francis King is treasurer of the Socialist History Society

Ben Pimlott (1945–2004)

I had the privilege of knowing Ben Pimlott in two capacities. First, from his frequent use of the Labour Party archives; secondly, as a student on his Master's degree course at Birkbeck College. There was some empathy between us, as we were both ex-public schoolboys of the same age, who found ourselves in the Labour Party.

It was indeed at Marlborough that he first displayed his flair for radical journalism, when he and James Curren (later to be editor of *New Socialist* and professor of Media Studies at Goldsmiths College) produced a humorous magazine called *Stroke*, so-called because Ben had been caned for not attending school chapel. However, in spite of his education he did not come from a conservative background. His father, J. A. R. Pimlott, was a civil servant and part-time historian, who published works on social history. He also thought up the idea of the polytechnics in 1968.

Throughout his life Ben pursued a triple career as academic, writer and politician. He stood as Labour candidate in Arundel in February 1974. In October 1974 and 1979 he stood as Labour candidate in Cleveland and Whitby, a seat that in a good Labour year he would have won. He was an active Fabian, serving on the society's executive from 1987 until he died. He was its Chair in 1993–94. I cannot, however, see Ben on the Labour front benches. He was far too nice a person.

Ben's first book *Labour and the Left in the 1930s*, about left-wing grass-roots activities in the years preceding the Second World War, was interesting in that it was written at the time when history was repeating itself with similar grass-roots activity in the 1970s and 1980s. His book on Dalton was monumental, winning the Whitbread prize. His biography of Harold Wilson, based on Labour Party press cuttings along with some interesting oral evidence, was better than the official one by Philip Ziegler. Most of us were surprised when his next work was a biography of the Queen. He did have an interest in the British constitution and it did display a breadth to his historical interests.

I lost touch with him in recent years, so I never sounded him out about his views on New Labour. He was anyway busy with his administrative work, as warden of Goldsmiths College. I did not agree with his ideas prior to Labour coming back to power on forging an anti-Conservative alliance with the Liberals. However, in spite of the few differences Ben and I might have had, I will always remember him as this highly intelligent, slightly shy Labour Party historian, who was not averse to hearing a bit of gossip.

Stephen Bird
National Museum of Labour History, Manchester

Forum
In search of Orwell

Few would dispute George Orwell's position in the lexicon of popular twentieth century novelists: indeed, *Nineteen Eighty-Four* was recently voted the nation's eighth favourite novel in the BBC's *The Big Read*. But socialists and socialist historians have yet to come up with a definitive answer to a more controversial question: what was Orwell's political significance? Here, John Newsinger and Andy Croft offer two possible perspectives on the debate.

The other Blair

The extent to which George Orwell can still excite controversy is amply demonstrated by Scott Lucas's new book, *The Betrayal of Dissent*.[1] This is, in the main, a well-deserved assault on the likes of Christopher Hitchens, Nick Cohen, David Aaronovitch, Johann Hari and John Lloyd for their support for US imperialism, but it is prefaced by two chapters that purport to reveal Orwell as the patron saint of traitors and renegades. They have merely continued what Orwell began with Hitchens, in particular, very self-consciously laying claim to Orwell's mantle. Unfortunately, the account of Orwell that Lucas provides is, taken as a whole, fundamentally flawed. It is an exercise in character assassination rather than an attempt at a critical understanding.

Now this is an important point because even when dealing with one's political enemies and opponents, and perhaps especially with them, one is surely obliged to take their arguments and concerns seriously. This Lucas signally fails to do as far as Orwell is concerned. Put simply, for Orwell, from 1936–7 onwards, the great question was the relationship between the left and Stalinism. His experiences in Spain together with his investigations into Soviet realities, led him to regard the destruction of 'the Soviet myth' as a priority for socialists. This concern informed his political thinking and activity up until his death. It is not possible to discuss Orwell seriously without confronting this central issue in his intellectual biography. And this is a confrontation that Lucas consistently refuses both in his biography of Orwell,[2] in his new book on 'Betrayal' and elsewhere.

In his new book, Lucas celebrates the anti-war demonstrations of 2003. It seems a fair assumption that a significant number of these who took part in these marches would have read at least some Orwell and that far from being repelled by the man's renegacy would have actually felt, as I do, that his legacy, for want of a better word, was with them rather than with Bush and Blair. There is a good reason for this: Orwell famously condemned both the British Empire and Stalinism. In November 1945, for example, he refused an invitation from the Duchess of Atholl to appear on a platform condemning Soviet policy in Eastern Europe because the organisers would not condemn British rule in India. He made the point that, however much he might hate Stalinism, he was a man of the left and would conduct his fight against Stalinism within the left. At much the same time, Orwell was also concerned to defend the right of the communist-led Greek resistance to take up arms against the British occupation of Greece.[3] The significance of all this is completely lost on Lucas. Admittedly, he does not condemn Orwell as a traitor for rejecting Stalinism as was once the case; what he does instead is ignore the whole question. For my money this makes Orwell's political development incomprehensible and it is out of this incomprehension that Lucas constructs his flawed portrait. For George Lucas the great traitor was 'Darth Vader', for Scott Lucas it is 'George Orwell'. The whole exercise subjects Orwell to the same methods that Lucas complains of when executed by the likes of Hitchens and co.

Orwell and socialism

Any serious consideration of Orwell has to start with his attitude towards Stalinism. This had two dimensions: his attitude towards British communists and towards the Soviet Union. Without any question he polemicised fiercely against British communists. As far as he was concerned they were, first and foremost, supporters of whatever line currently emanated from Moscow, would routinely defend and justify the most appalling crimes and, consequently, were a pernicious influence on the left. This was not the whole truth, of course, but it was nevertheless the part of the truth that gave shape to the whole. Whereas in the Soviet Union and in Eastern Europe the crimes of Stalinism cost millions of lives, in Britain the crime of Stalinism was to involve many of the best on the Left in apologising for or covering up mass murder. It was Edward Thompson, for example, in an article on William Morris no less, who, in 1951, dismissed allegations of tyranny in Eastern

Europe as 'the Big Lie technique of Goebbels over again'. Indeed, this was apparently a lie 'so monstrous that we cannot be troubled with it, we turn our backs on it, and divert the argument on to more practical questions'.[4] Of course, it was Thompson who was guilty of endorsing 'the Big Lie technique of Goebbels over again' and at a time when good communists were being imprisoned, tortured and executed in their thousands across Eastern Europe. Let me emphasise that Thompson is not singled out here as part of any Lucas-style character assassination, but precisely because he was one of the finest of the CPGB's intellectuals.

Orwell, of course, attempted to expose 'the Big Lie' within the left. On one occasion, he remarked in the journal Polemic that he had in his possession a pamphlet about the Russian Revolution written by Maxim Litvinov in 1918. This made no mention at all of Stalin but did praise Trotsky, Zinoviev, Kamenev and others. What, Orwell asked, would be the attitude of a good communist to this? The pamphlet would either have to be suppressed or rewritten with references to Stalin added and those to Trotsky and others removed. Although Orwell did not make the point, possession of such a pamphlet would actually have been a political offence in Stalin's Russia, and might well cost the owner his or her life in a labour camp. Interestingly enough, when Randall Swingler replied for the CPGB to Orwell's attacks in Polemic, he claimed that the usefulness of Litvinov's pamphlet 'has been superseded and its account of events modified in subsequent histories of wider authenticity'.[5] The histories to which he referred were, of course, those that took cognisance of the Moscow Trials. Once again Swingler is singled out precisely because he was one of the party's best.

The other dimension to Orwell's hostility to Stalinism was his attempt to understand the class nature of the Soviet Union. He refused to accept that the tyranny that existed in Russia could be legitimately described as socialism and inevitably came into contact with Trotskyist critiques of the Soviet order. The theory of bureaucratic collectivism, advocated by some American Trotskyists, had the most influence on his thinking. Whatever degree of validity this theory had, it does show how seriously Orwell took the issue of Stalinism. Moreover, he rejected the Soviet system not because it was socialist, but precisely because it was not socialist—was indeed the opposite of socialism. And, of course, he was absolutely right. This is not to say that he did not make mistakes, in the case of his relationship with the Information Research Department (IRD) a serious and unforgiveable mistake, but nevertheless his stance, taken as a whole, is certainly a commendable one when compared with that of those on the left who continued praising Stalin right up until his successor told them to stop.

What of Orwell and the IRD? The evidence, in my opinion, points to Orwell being a dupe. He believed that he was associating himself with a pro-paganda organisation established by Clement Attlee's Labour government to oppose Stalinism from a social-democratic position and had no notion of its connections with M16.[6] His misjudgement can be partly explained by his poor health, but more important are his illusions in the Labour gov-ernment and his hostility to Stalinism. The theory of bureaucratic collectivism lent itself to the notion that Stalinism was worse than capital-ism and this was certainly one aspect of the way his political thinking was developing when he died. His stated support for the United States in the event of a Third World War is evidence of this. But there were other aspects to his development as well and at the time of this death he had certainly not surrendered to the right. In September 1949, on his death-bed, he signed a statement that appeared in Tribune setting up a committee to help those Spaniards in exile or in Franco's prisons (including communists). The other signatories included Albert Camus, Jean Paul Sartre, Andre Gide, André Breton and Stephen Spender.[7] Orwell's position at this time was quite admirable: he was opposed to the imprisonment and execution of com-munists by both Franco *and* Stalin. The CPGB, of course, only opposed their execution by Franco. Moreover Orwell remained as opponent of any British McCarthyism until his death. The reason that *Animal Farm* and *Nineteen Eighty Four* were posthumously, repeat posthumously, confiscated by the right was not because their author had abandoned socialism, but because so many on the left continued to have illusions in Stalinism. With Orwell removed from the scene this allowed the two volumes to be used to hammer the left. He was already taking steps to prevent this happening when he died.

The July–August 1947 issue of the American journal *Partisan Review* pub-lished Orwell's article, 'Towards European Unity' as part of a series on 'The Future of Socialism'. The other contributors were Sidney Hook, Arthur Schlesinger Jnr, Granville Hicks and Victor Serge. In his contribution, Orwell argued that the situation confronting socialists was pretty grim. At a time when there was a Labour government, with a strong parliamentary majority, in power in London, when there were powerful mass communist parties in France and Italy, and when the Soviet Union had a complete dom-ination over Eastern Europe, Orwell nevertheless insisted that the odds were very much against the successful establishment of socialism. More likely was an extended period of war and tyranny with the likelihood of the world being divided between unassailable superstates, two or three empires, armed with nuclear weapons that would keep humanity down for centuries. This prospect was, of course, the inspiration for *Nineteen Eighty Four*. The only way to avoid catastrophe was for democratic socialism to be established in a large area of the world and he considered Western Europe as offering the best prospect. Consequently, for Orwell in 1947, 'a socialist United States of Europe seems to me the only worth-while political objective today'.

This socialist United States of Europe would, he warned, be opposed by the Soviet Union, and the malign influence of the domestic communists, taking their lead from Moscow, would have to be fought against. It would be opposed by the United States, with Britain being a particular problem because it was already 'almost a dependency of the USA'. Such a socialist Europe would have to renounce imperialism, something unlikely to be accomplished 'without bloodshed'. And, he foresaw the Catholic church, at least on the continent, as providing a rallying point for the forces of conservatism. On balance, the forces opposed to a socialist Europe were considerably stronger than those in favour. Nevertheless, socialism was the only way forward if barbarism was to be avoided. Despite his pessimism, Orwell did recognise that the situation was not fixed, that circumstances could change. There was always the possibility that 'a powerful socialist movement might arise in the United States' and, if nuclear war could be avoided, he thought that by the 1960s there would 'be millions of young Russians…eager for more freedom'. This from the author of *Nineteen Eighty Four*. Looked at realistically, however, the situation in 1947 did not provide much occasion for optimism.[8]

There was much to recommend this analysis at the time. It was an attempt to understand the situation before him of a committed socialist who had long since recognised the Soviet Union as a murderous tyranny, was a staunch opponent of British imperialism and never believed that the Labour Party was going to accomplish a socialist transformation. He never surrendered these beliefs and despite the enormous odds argued that socialism was the only cause worth fighting for until his death.

Orwell today

This rehearsal of his 1947 article is necessary because there are still those who would deny either that Orwell ever was a socialist or that he remained one in 1947. What of his significance for socialists and socialist historians today? Obviously the world has moved on considerably since Orwell's death. The communist dictatorships in Eastern Europe and the Soviet Union have gone; Western capitalism has not collapsed, as Orwell thought likely; and the reformist Labour Party, that he had supported as the best that was possible at the time, has become Tony Blair's conservative New Labour. Orwell's recognition, in 1947, of Britain as 'almost a dependency of the USA' has been grotesquely realised with British participation in the US attack on Iraq earlier this year. In the circumstances we can only admire the astonishing prescience that led Orwell to change his name from Blair.

What would Orwell have made of developments since his death? There is, of course, no way of knowing. What we can know, however, is what he thought about developments while he was alive. This involves recognition of the way that his ideas developed. Indeed, the only way to understand his ideas is to regard them as a process of intellectual development that was unfortunately cut short when he was only forty-six. Would he have remained a dissident socialist or would he have joined with Koestler, Dwight Macdonald and others in abandoning the socialist cause. We have no way of knowing beyond the judgements we make regarding his life. To me, at any rate, it is inconceivable, that Orwell would not in 1956 have opposed both the Anglo-French-Israeli invasion of Egypt and the Soviet invasion of Hungary. This is guesswork, however, but if he had defected to the right it would have involved a rupture in his politics rather than some sort of culmination.

What of Orwell's relevance today. His attitude towards imperialism is still unfortunately all too relevant. He regarded imperialism as a system of theft with the police and military holding the victim down while the businessman went through his pockets. It is hard to think of a better characterisation of the US occupation of Iraq. He had, of course, been a colonial police officer in Burma and so had no illusions whatever regarding the routine brutalities of colonial rule. One of the things he found particularly objectionable was the way that language was distorted to disguise actions people would otherwise regard as unacceptable: 'pacification' for the bombing of defenceless villages. The systematic dishonesty with which New Labour prepared the way for the attack on Iraq would have come as no surprise and he would have found the intimate relationship between the Blair government and the Murdoch press no more than was to be expected from a party that has so enthusiastically embraced plutocracy. Clearly for socialists, imperialism is once again at the top of the agenda, together with the domestic policies that it sustains and is sustained by.

More problematic is Orwell's attitude towards feminism and women's liberation. The best critique of Orwell from a feminist perspective is still Daphne Patai's *The Orwell Mystique* published nearly twenty years ago.[9] While her assault is too one-sided for my money, hers is certainly one of the most important books on Orwell and should not be forgotten in the current

Orwell revival. The relevance of Orwell's attitude towards women's liberation is that he was wrong. While he sided with the underdog in Spain and
the empire, while he stood by the victims of Stalinism, while he identified
himself with the miners and the unemployed in Britain, as far as women's
liberation and women's equality were concerned he never broke with the
patriarchal attitudes and prejudices of the time. Patai's account does not adequately situate him in this context and is positively unfair to him on a number
of occasions, but nevertheless she serves up a timely warning against the
male socialist who opposes all oppression except that of women.[10]

John Newsinger

Notes

1. Scott Lucas, *The Betrayal of Dissent: Beyond Orwell, Hitchens and the New American
   Century* (London, 2004).
2. Scott Lucas, *Orwell* (London, 2003).
3. See John Newsinger, Orwell's Politics (Basingstoke, 1999), pp.17, 106–7.
4. Cited in John Callaghan, *Cold War, Crisis and Conflict. The CPGB 1951–1968*
   (London, 2003), p.89.
5. Newsinger, *Orwell's Politics*, pp.144–5. In his biography of Swingler, Andy Croft
   has him remarking 'in mock dismay' while on a disillusioning visit to
   Czechoslovakia in 1953 that 'Orwell was right after all!': Andy Croft, *Comrade
   Heart. A Life of Randall Swingler* (Manchester, 2003), p. 219.
6. In his *Betrayal*, Lucas insists that Orwell 'offered up' names to M16 (p.30) and
   cites Andy Croft's association of Orwell's actions with the blacklisting of
   Randall Swingler that he made in a letter to the *Guardian* in 2002 (pp.52–3). Of
   course, Orwell did not hand names over to M16, but to the IRD which he
   believed to be a propaganda agency set up to support the Labour government.
   Lucas's claim is a shabby smear of the very kind that he finds so objectionable
   when carried out by Christopher Hitchens or Nick Cohen against the anti-war
   movement. As for M15 having to be told by Orwell that Randall Swingler was
   a communist, this seems highly unlikely and Andy Croft does not repeat it in
   his biography of Swingler.
7. George Orwell, *Our Job Is To Make Life Worth Living 1949–1950* (London, 1998),
   p.164.
8. The neglect of this crucial article in studies of Orwell is really rather surprising. See Newsinger, *Orwell's Politics*, pp.150–4.
9. Daphne Patai, *The Orwell Mystique* (Amherst, 1986).
10. In a footnote, Lucas refers to me as having casually dismissed 'feminist quib-
    bles' regarding Orwell as 'fundamentally wrongheaded'. This is really quite
    outrageous. The quote comes from my rejection of Patai's claim that *Burmese
    Days* was a novel about masculinity rather than about imperialism. I still think
    she was wrong about this. Nevertheless, despite my disagreement with Patai on

a number of points, I insist that her book is 'one of the most interesting recent accounts of Orwell's work' (pp.8–9), something I have repeated elsewhere, and regularly insist on to students. Moreover, I go on to lament that Orwell's social-ism 'never led him to question the notions of masculinity and of male supremacy that had been bred into him...a serious and damaging criticism' (p.48). Some casual dismissal. Lucas's footnote, the only reference in his vol-ume to my extensive and continuing work on Orwell, manages to casually distort my argument.

A sack of potatoes or freedom fries?
Orwell in the twenty-first century

Tom Paulin's most recent book, *The Invasion Handbook*, consists of a series of thumbnail sketches in verse of key moments in European history between the wars, from Versailles to Munich, Jarrow to Dunkirk. The Spanish Civil War is represented in the book by the following prose-poem:

> Eileen got papers and passports ready. She distributed the money she was holding for various ILP members who were still at large, and met the three in the station at the last possible moment before the train left for France. Incredibly, the train had left early. So they hid out a third night and then made for the station again. They smiled and spoke cheerfully and confi-dently like happy tourists or delegates returning from a lively conference.[1]

For readers of Bernard Crick's life of Orwell this passage may seem familiar:

> Eileen, having got papers and passports together, and paid back personal money she was holding for various ILP members still at large, met them at the station at the last possible moment before the evening train left for France—which they then found, incredibly for Spain, had left early. So a third night was spent hiding out before the four of then got on the morn-ing train together and sat confidently in the restaurant car, as if they were tourists or delegates returning from some conference.[2]

As history is filtered for twenty-first century readers through poem, biog-raphy and memoir, it is clear that Orwell's version of events in Spain is no longer a competing, contested account. It is the only one. His flight from Barcelona is 'Spain'. The canonisation of the writer whom Tosco Fyvel once called 'saintly' requires that his writings are not merely canonical, but the canon itself. Of all the thousands of eye-witness accounts, novels and memoirs written about the participation of British volunteers in Spain, only *Homage to Catalonia* has been filmed. Northern Stage's recent adaptation of the book for the theatre (following their acclaimed staging of *Animal Farm* and *Nineteen Eighty-Four*) summarises events in Spain as a moment when

> thousands of ordinary men and women travelled to Spain to fight in the Spanish Civil War because they believed they could change the world. Amongst them was a young idealist, George Orwell, struggling to find a utopian vision himself. But somehow it went wrong.

There is no room in this simplified narrative for Franco or fascism or 'Non-Intervention' or even the Spanish people. This was a utopian war about 'changing the world', not the defence of democracy ; a war fought by foreign idealists, rather than ordinary Spaniards. Was the Spanish Civil War lost because it 'went wrong' ? Or did it go 'wrong' because it was lost ? And who or what was 'lost' ? The cause of Spanish democracy, or the utopian vision of George Orwell ? The process by which a major European civil war can be so easily reduced to the syllogism, 'change the world', 'George Orwell', 'went wrong' must make any historian uncomfortable.

Last year, the centenary of Orwell's birth, we were treated to two new breeze-block biographies (for a man who insisted he wanted no biography at all, Orwell has so far enjoyed the attentions of at least five biographers). Turner prize-winner Rachel Whiteread made a plaster-cast of room 101 at Broadcasting House for the V&A. *Nineteen Eighty-Four* was voted the nation's eighth favourite novel in the BBC's *The Big Read*. There was much media excitement at newly-discovered film footage of the young Eric Blair at Eton. Meanwhile the latest CGI technology has been employed on US television to produce a *Babe*-like animated *Animal Farm* (with Patrick Stewart providing the voice of Napoleon). There are now half a million internet sites containing references to 'Orwell'. As Pasternak observed when Mayakovsky was posthumously declared by Stalin to be the leading poet of the revolution, it was as if he had been 'dumped on the public like a sack of potatoes'.

In his absurd and embarrassing hagiography, *Orwell's Victory*, Hitchens writes about a man who 'faced the competing orthodoxies of his day with little more than a battered type-writer and a stubborn personality', who 'had dirt under his fingernails and an understanding of the rhythms of nature' and who, 'when Spain was menaced by fascism he was among the first to shoulder a rifle and feel the weight of a pack'. For Hitchens, Orwell was a 'flinty and solitary loner' defending 'sturdy English virtues', 'a modest man', 'proud but by no means vain', 'as English as roast beef and warm beer'. The

pages of *Orwell's Victory* are thick with the terms of heavy-handed praise—
'genius', 'insight', 'principles', 'independence', 'prescient conviction',
'pioneering insistence', 'clarity and courage', 'integrity', 'intellectual honesty',
'vindicated by time', 'cleverly anticipated', 'essential clarity', 'uncommonly
prescient', 'truth-telling', 'vividly contemporary', 'dangerously truthful'.[3]

For Hitchens, Orwell was 'one of the founders of the discipline of post-
colonialism', a 'libertarian before the word had gained currency' and a writer
who 'pioneered' cultural studies. He was 'one of the founding fathers of anti-
communism' (credited with inventing the term 'Cold War'), who 'anticipated'
the collapse of the Soviet Union and whose Wigan notebooks 'would not
have disgraced Friedrich Engels'. Elsewhere he is a writer whose work 'prefigured' postwar British 'Angry' fiction, who 'helped keep alive the socialist
press in England' and who made 'the only English contribution to the literature of twentieth-century totalitarianism'. You half expect Hitchens to
flourish a 'curiously prescient' prediction of the 'War Against Terrorism', the
sacking of Gerard Houllier or the winner of the next series of *Big Brother*
(curiously, one contribution to contemporary culture which no-one wants
to claim for Orwell). Like Nostradamus—and of course Christopher
Hitchens—Orwell was never wrong.

I used to think it was possible to engage with 'Orwell', that his works were
there to be read and re-read, enjoyed and disliked, criticised and taught—
just like those of any twentieth-century writer. I interviewed the novelist Jack
Hilton shortly before his death in 1983. A plasterer by trade, Hilton was
blacklisted in the 1920s because of his activities in the National Association
of Operative Plasterers, then bound over in the early 1930s because of his
involvement in the activities of the National Unemployed Workers'
Movement in Rochdale. His autobiography *Caliban Shrieks* (1935) was first
published in the *Adelphi*, where it was favourably reviewed by Orwell. Hilton
told me the extraordinary story of how, when Victor Gollancz commis-
sioned Orwell to write a book about poverty in the depressed areas, he asked
Hilton if he could stay with him in Rochdale. Hilton refused, urging Orwell
instead to visit the miners of Wigan:

> So George went to Wigan and he might have stayed away. He wasted
> money, energy and wrote piffle…George wanted to get at the pith and
> he didn't know how, and failed…and the fatheads of readers, unassoci-
> ated with what can be done in art about the rough stuff of prole life, got
> a colour that wasn't worth the paint mixes. Authenticity, in the sense of
> Wiganers and Wigan, was travestied…George was a baby empiric imp,

making the most out of a limited experience. Giving a picture grotesque: false to the general whole. So this was Wigan. The Wigan of forty nights sleep above a tripe shop.[4]

Of course, Jack Hilton is not even mentioned in Gordon Bowker's new biography of 'one of the greatest writers of the twentieth century'.[5]

A few years later, I came across an unpublished 1937 letter from George Orwell among Randall Swingler's papers. It was his 'lost' reply to Nancy Cunard's famous questionnaire on the Spanish Civil War, one which critics had routinely assumed was 'suppressed' by Cunard and Swingler (who published the questionnaire). It was, to say the least, an interesting letter (and one which Orwell clearly did not intend for publication), intemperate and offensive, accusing Cunard of looking after her 'dirty little dividends' in defending democracy in Spain, abusing Stephen Spender and Auden as 'fashionable pansies' and attacking the Spanish republican government for 'rivetting' fascism on the Spanish working-class. When I offered the letter in the *New Statesman* I imagined that it might lead to some re-assessment of Orwell's developing analysis of the war in Spain; instead I was denounced in the letters pages over the following weeks as a 'Stalinist', while the Orwell estate threatened to claim for breach of copyright.[6]

Elsewhere I have proposed that *Nineteen Eighty-Four* owed many of its details and much of its political originality to a forgotten feminist dystopia by 'Murray Constantine' (Katherine Burdekin) *Swastika Night* (1937). This is not a question of plagiarism, but of recognising that the intellectual sources of *Nineteen Eighty-Four* go rather further than Zamyatin and Huxley. Considering the feminist criticisms of the novel, its relation to Burdekin's might be thought to deserve some consideration. The collection in which I first made this argument however, was simply dismissed by Timothy Garton Ash in the *TLS* as 'sloppy, low-grade sniping', 'the authentic voice of Eeyore'.[7] Although D. J. Taylor acknowledges the extraordinary similarities between the two novels in his new life of Orwell, he rejects this kind of 'influence-mongering' on the grounds that *Nineteen Eighty-Four* came out of a decade of political activity, and not because Orwell 'browsed through an obscure novel that came his way through the Left Book Club'.[8] But feminist arguments about Orwell are routinely dealt with by this sleight of hand which moves from a discussion of the books to the life. Christopher Hitchens dismisses feminist critics of Orwell like Bea Campbell, Deirdre Beddoe and Janet Montefiore with a stern reminder that that no-one who enjoyed the company of tough-minded women (and who married two of them) can really have been much of a misogynist.

Wigan, Spain, *Nineteen Eighty-Four*—these were key moments in the invention of 'Orwell', each of which was, I believe, more complex and more interesting than conventional biographical accounts suggest. But Orwell enthusiasts have their sack of potatoes and they certainly don't want to have to go through the sack looking for the bruised or rotten ones. The poet Arnold Rattenbury once told me how he and the other editors of *Our Time* were once pelted with rotten vegetables by Orwell and the Canadian poet Paul Potts when they left King Street; trying to contribute to Orwell scholarship feels a bit like that.

As a novelist, Orwell was a minor figure. No-one took him seriously as a novelist before the Cold War. *A Clergyman's Daughter*, *Keep the Aspidistra Flying* and *Coming Up for Air* are minor novels by any standard, undistinguished and adolescent attempts at the game of *epater les bourgeois*. As portraits of the English middle classes between the wars, they do not bear comparison with novels by, say, Patrick Hamilton, Virginia Woolf or J.B. Priestley. The initial success of *Animal Farm* and *Nineteen Eighty-Four* had rather less to do with 'literary merit' than with their assiduous promotion by the CIA and its cultural arms in the early years of the Cold War. There is a compelling case to be made for a writer whom H.G. Wells once called a 'Trotskyite with big feet' belonging to a native Trotskyite political tradition, one which has not been notable for its imaginative writers. As ex-Trotskyist Christopher Hitchens has put it, Orwell's writings are 'the most English form in which cosmopolitan and subversive Trotskyism has ever been cast'. But you can't pick and choose your Orwell. If *Animal Farm* and *Nineteen Eighty-Four* are Trotskyist political fictions, rather than simply anti-communist ones, then those who inhabit that tradition must find ways of accommodating their author's snobbery, casual anti-semitism, occasional misogyny and what often seems uncommonly like misanthropy.

As a political thinker, Orwell changed his opinions so often (though always with the zeal of the converted) that it is difficult to know what his political thought amounted to, except as a series of negatives. This may make him immensely quotable, but also leaves his writings open to abuse. In any case, was Orwell right to propose armed resistance to Churchill at the beginning of the Second World War? Or to argue that fascism and 'so-called democracy' are like Tweededum and Tweedledee? Or to describe the Spanish republic as a *fascist* government? Orwell's fondness for political *volte-face* was matched only by an intense dislike of it in others. The fact that other people changed their opinions less often allowed him to dramatise himself as a heroic dissident and everyone else as craven disciples of fashion or orthodoxy. The important thing was not to be consistent but to be contrary.

The one consistent element in Orwell's thinking—his 'premature' anti-Stalinism—was an honourable, if unoriginal, position. It led him to make exaggerated and wildly inaccurate attacks on individuals (for example, the assault on Auden in *Inside the Whale*). It often elided into crude anti-communism. It delivered him into the hands of the cold warriors in British Intelligence. And 'Stalinism' still needs unpicking if it is to be anything more than a term of blanket abuse. Tommy Jackson, for example—by temperament and circumstances a natural rebel and a constant thorn in the side of King Street—introduced his wonderful *Old Friends to Keep* (1950) (a study of Jane Austen, Bunyan, George Eliot, Fielding, Dickens etc) by cheerfully describing himself as a 'Stalinist, a Marxist and an English Humanist'. Nevertheless, Orwell's critique of those western intellectuals who voluntarily subordinated their political judgement, their common-sense and their common decency to their admiration for the Stalin dictatorship was a profoundly important one. The characters of O'Brien in *Nineteen Eighty-Four* and Minimus and Squealer in *Animal Farm* are major fictional creations, utterly recognisable and terrifying studies in the intellectual temptations of Power. For this, if nothing else, Orwell deserves to be remembered and read and re-read.

However, anti-Stalinism (like anti-communism) has as much resonance now as Milton's anti-Catholicism or Luther's anti-semitism. The monsters of the new century may be authoritarian, Machiavellian and repulsive, but it makes no sense to describe them as Stalinists. Of course, some writers and intellectuals are still attracted to power and its rewards. There are still plenty of would-be Squealers prepared to present literary differences as ideological ones, to change their opinions at the drop of a hat, launch *ad hominem* attacks on their opponents as knaves or fools, and to endorse the rich and powerful. But, as Scott Lucas has painstakingly demonstrated in *The Betrayal of Dissent*, it is precisely those champions of 'Orwell' in the twentieth-century who most closely resemble the character of Squealer. Unpleasant polemicists like Julie Burchill, Melanie Phillips, Paul Johnson, David Aaronovitch, Christopher Hitchens and Peter Hitchens are all Orwell's children. Untroubled by doubt or memory, they long ago exchanged accuracy and consistency for pugnacious generalisation and dreadful over-writing. Outspoken in their condemnation of Sin, rain during Wimbledon and short-sighted referees, they bravely defend the powerful against the weak. Like Orwell they trail their socialist credentials to legitimise their attacks on the Left. And like Orwell, they are never wrong.

In Hitchens's account Orwell was always right and everyone else is a fool, or worse—their motivations 'stupid', 'sinister', 'silly' or 'credulous'. The arguments of Edward Thompson (whose 'Outside the Whale' is still arguably the best essay on Orwell), Salman Rushdie, Edward Said, Isaac Deutscher, Conor Cruise O'Brien and the 'sub-literate' Raymond Williams are denounced as expressions of 'Orwell-hatred', 'too stupid or too compromised', unable to forgive Orwell for 'giving ammunition to the enemy'. Moreover, Hitchens claims that 'Orwell' would 'have seen straight through the characters who chant "No War on Iraq"'. Barbara Amiel recently told readers of the *Daily Telegraph* that 'Orwell' must have written the EU Constitution. A few years ago, one commentator suggested that every British soldier involved in the invasion of Afghanistan should be given a copy of Orwell's *Collected Essays* to take with them (though presumably not the twenty-volume *Collected Works* currently selling for £850 a set). Labour Party chair Dave Trieseman had obviously been reading *Inside the Whale* when he argued that the British left should support the invasion of Iraq on the grounds that in the 1930s the appeasement of Hitler *by the left* had failed. Helen Liddell, meanwhile, compared the US-British invasion of Iraq to those who, like Orwell, volunteered to fight in Spain. Revelations that Orwell named names to an arm of British Intelligence have done nothing to temper the myth of Saint George or to cool the intellectual and publishing industry surrounding it. Hitchens, for example, believes that 'too much has been made of this trivial episode'. Nevertheless he defends Orwell's actions on the grounds that the IRD was not involved in domestic surveillance, that Orwell was not motivated by personal gain, that nobody suffered as a result, and that, anyway, some of his suspicions turned out to be *right*. If Orwell were revealed tomorrow to have been a member of a neo-Nazi satanic paedophile ring, the usual apologists would crawl out from under their stones with their little justifications and offerings to the saint.[9]

This is not to argue that it is impossible to 'reclaim' Orwell for the left in the twentieth-first century. Books have a life of their own and it is not possible to legislate for the ways in which new readers will make use of them. In the prison where I worked until recently as writer-in-residence, I met a young man who had embarked on a crash-course of self-directed political reading. In a matter of weeks he had worked his way from Ben Elton and Ian Banks to Michael Moore, Chomsky and Plato. By the time he came across *Nineteen Eighty-Four*, it seemed to him an entertainingly precise anatomy of the Bush-Blair 'War on Terror', particularly its abuse of news, language and memory. In the USA, anti-Bush web-sites include the spoof-Republican 'Bush Orwell 04' and the satirical Students for an Orwellian Society ('because 2004 is 20 years too late'). On the other hand, the ready availability these days of *Nineteen Eighty-Four* (as a 'classic') in Moscow bookshops does not appear to have done much to strengthen the forces of liberalism in the new Russia.

George Orwell was once a man, a man moreover in constant intellectual movement, a man in flight who liked picking a good fight. 'George Orwell' became a biographical disguise, a literary character and a shifting ideological space. He changed his opinions, his allegiances, his friends, his class, even his name. During the Cold War 'Orwell' acquired a specific political significance that stabilised—although it also narrowed—the meaning of his life and writings. Since the end of the Cold War, however, it is clear that 'Orwell' has been increasingly emptied of meaning and uprooted from History. Like the collection of displaced statues outside the New Tretyakov gallery in Moscow, Orwell is an icon torn out of historical context. And like all public monuments, 'Orwell' is now a temptingly blank space on which the careless, mischievous and mendacious can scribble whatever they want.

Andy Croft

Notes

1. Tom Paulin, *The Invasion Handbook* (London, 2002), p.113.
2. Bernard Crick, *Orwell: a life* (London, 1980), p.225.
3. Christopher Hitchens, *Orwell's Victory* (London, 2002).
4. Feeling partly responsible for *The Road to Wigan Pier*, Jack Hilton replied with a very different travel-book, the once-acclaimed *English Ways* (1940); for Hilton see 'The itch of class: essays in memory of Jack Hilton', *Middlesex Polytechnic History Journal*, spring 1985 and Andy Croft, *Red Letter Days* (London, 1990).
5. Gordon Bowker, *George Orwell* (London, 2003), p.xi.
6. 'The Awkward Squaddie', *New Statesman and Society*, 18 March 1994.
7. Christopher Norris (ed.), *Inside the Myth. Orwell: views from the left* (London, 1984); Timothy Garton Ash, *TLS*, 8 February 1985.
8. D. J. Taylor, *Orwell: The Life* (London, 2003), p.376.
9. Hitchens, *Orwell's Victory*, p.118, originally published in E. P. Thompson (ed.), *Out of Apathy* (London, 1960); 'Outside the Whale' was collected in *The Poverty of Theory and Other Essays* (London, 1978).

Reviews

Books to be remembered (9)

Lytton Strachey, *Eminent Victorians* (1918)

Lytton Strachey was born in 1880, the son of an army General. He was educated privately and then at Cambridge. As a young man Strachey was a lively and intimate member of the Bloomsbury group, whose members included E.M. Forster, Virginia Woolf and J.M. Keynes.

Strachey began writing and publishing as a young man, and his first book was published in 1912. This was *Landmarks in French Literature*, received with only a modest public notice. It was six years later, in 1918, that the first edition of *Eminent Victorians* appeared, and it immediately became widely influential. He followed this with a biography of Queen Victoria in 1921 and *Elizabeth and Essex* in 1928. He died in 1932, and *Eminent Victorians* was republished with only minor emendations by Penguin Books in 1948. It has since been reprinted several times.

Together with Strachey's essay on Florence Nightingale, which is discussed below, the volume included similar length essays on Cardinal Manning, Thomas Arnold and General Gordon. Lytton Strachey made his purpose in writing these essays abundantly clear: 'The art of biography seems to have fallen on evil times in England. We have had, it is true, a few masterpieces, but we have never had, like the French, a great biographical tradition; we have had no Fontenells and Condorcets, with their incomparable *éloges*, compressing into a few shining pages the manifold existences of men…we do not reflect that it is perhaps as difficult to write a good life as to live one.' And he continued to exhibit what he thought was too often the style and content of English biography: 'Those two fat volumes, with which it is our custom to commemmorate the dead—who does not know them, with their ill-digested masses of material, their slip-shod style, their tone of tedious panegyris, their lamentable lack of selection, of detachment, of design? They are as familiar as the *cortège* of the undertaker, and wear the same air of slow, funereal barbarism…'

Strachey's four biographical essays provide interesting and at times striking examples of his rewriting of famous lives. I have chose the essay on Florence Nightingale to illustrate his approach, mainly because she is probably the best known character of his four subjects. He opens his chapter: 'Every one knows the popular conception of Florence Nightingale. The saintly, self-sacrificing women, the delicate maiden of high degree who threw aside the pleasures of a life of ease to succour the afflicted, the Lady with the Lamp, gliding through the horrors of the hospital at Scutari, and consecrating with the radiance of her goodness the dying soldier's couch—the vision is familiar to all. But the truth was different…in the real Miss Nightingale there was more that was interesting than in the legendary one; there was also less that was agreeable.'

She came from an extremely well-to-do family, living in a large country house in Derbyshire with another in the New Forest, and rooms in Mayfair for the London season. All young women in her social class were expected to marry, but not Florence. She was remarkably unhappy and unsettled in her younger years and she began to think of those outside her family life who were ill and sick, and who needed help. On travel round Britain and in Europe she began visiting hospitals, and this unknown to her family; she tried to enter Salisbury hospital for several months as a nurse, but was rebuffed by her family. Finally, in her early thirties she became superintendent of a charitable nursing home in Harley St. A year later the Crimean War began, and the ghastly condition of the facilities of the sick and wounded soon became known to the British public. Florence now had the opportunity she wanted; and she was fortunate. A close friend was Sidney Herbert who was at the War Office and in the cabinet, and when Florence offered her services, she was accepted. She arrived in Scutari, a suburb of Constantinople, in early November 1854, ten days before Balaclava, the day before the battle of Inkerman. With her were two personal attendants and thirty-eight nurses.

Her story has often been told, but what is often missed is the tenacity and persistence of her many confrontations with the medical and administrative staff of the army; and of the consequences for her own health. When she finally returned to England, she nearly died. The Royal Commission on health in the army, which was later established, involved quite major battles to achieve a balanced personnel and sensible objectives, and her *Notes affecting the Health, Efficiency and Hospital Administration of the British Army* were to be a major factor in the deliberations of the commission. Strachey provides considerable detail of her struggles against the obduracy of many of the army's leading officials and administrators but for around twenty years after the end of the war she remained an important influence upon medical affairs within the War Office. But only a woman of great moral strength and very considerable physical endurance would have been able to achieve what she accomplished; although, as Strachey notes: 'Succeeding Secretaries of State managed between them to undo a good deal of what had been accomplished, they could not undo it all.'

Florence Nightingale continued to work on conditions in hospitals and on sanitary work of all kinds. She lived in a small house in London and died in her ninety-first year. A remarkable life, told by Strachey in an interesting as well as iconoclastic volume.

John Saville

Richard Steigmann-Gall, *The Holy Reich. Nazi Conceptions of Christianity, 1919–1945* (Cambridge, Cambridge University Press, 2003), ISBN 0-521-82371-4, 310pp., £25.

In the early years of the Second World War, Hitler talked of his plans to crush Germany's churches. Such an intention fits well with an understanding of the Third Reich as totalitarian, determined to destroy not only left-wing power bases but any sites of potential opposition to a one-party state. But Nazi hostility to the churches went deeper than its distrust of the army or other conservative elites. For the SS leader Heinrich Himmler, for Hitler's influential secretary Martin Bormann and, apparently, for Hitler himself, Germany needed a new explicitly racial religion.

Yet many German Protestants and some Catholics voted for the Nazis, and members of both confessions could be found within the party. Its programme proclaimed that it stood for 'positive Christianity' and in the 1920s, Hitler even declared that the Nazis' goal was to complete the work that Christ had begun. How are we to understand this contradiction, that the Nazis claimed fealty to Christianity yet sought to destroy it? For many historians, the answer lies in the Nazis' deceit. The Third Reich was engaged in a war against Christianity and any claims to the contrary were simply false. Richard Steigmann-Gall, however, argues for another interpretation. Nazism, he holds, cannot be understood as inherently antagonistic to Christianity. Instead, for many of its members, it was shaped by Christianity.

More precisely, in many ways Nazism was shaped by Protestantism. Where Nazism denounced the Catholic Church as both alien and internationalising, Protestantism was seen as rightly resisting Rome and rooted in German history. Thus the Nazis enjoyed the support of the militant Protestant League and included Protestant pastors in its ranks while at the beginning of the 1930s members of the party formed the German Christians, a grouping which campaigned for a specifically Nazi Protestantism. Members of the German Christians, who ultimately failed in their efforts to take over Protestantism, claimed that Christ had not been Jewish but Aryan. They also argued that the Old Testament should be discarded as Jewish. These beliefs, Steigmann-Gall demonstrates, originated in German Protestantism. Likewise, the Nazis' denunciations of capitalism and calls for a 'third way' between liberalism and Marxism also strongly resonated with the pronouncements of some of the country's leading Protestants. Most strikingly, even those Nazis who explicitly disavowed Christianity appear to have been more favourable to aspects of it than we might expect. Thus for Alfred Rosenberg, often seen as Nazism's philospher, Christ was presented favourably while for the German Faith Movement, a pro-Nazi pagan grouping set up at the beginning of the 1930s, Catholicism was the enemy, Protestantism an admirable but ultimately ineffective protest against Rome.

The Holy Reich is an impressively researched work which has been praised by some of the leading historians whose views it criticises. It shows how both in public and private leading Nazis argued for the essential Christianity of Nazism. Hitler's denunciation of the churches, it argues, only came after the failure to capture Protestantism and needs to be seen in light of that frustration. But Nazism continued to see itself as close to Protestantism, and in one of its most striking elements, the book argues that Nazi paganism has been misunderstood, both in its ambition and its influence. Rosenberg sought to secure paganism's position as a third confession, not the only one, while Himmler insisted that those SS men who continued to adhere to Christianity should be regarded as favourably as those who, like him, had abandoned it. As for Hitler himself, he was critical of paganism in the party. Erich Ludendorff, a leading Nazi in the early period, was expelled in part because his religious views were seen as incompatible with a movement which sought to win Christians, while, as is well known, Hitler was deeply critical of Rosenberg's views, and, as is less familiar, distanced himself from Himmler's too. Paganism, in this argument, was not dominant in the regime, but just one strand of it, and an often harried one at that.

It is here, amidst a vast array of fascinating and illuminating material, that more needs to be said, not over influence, but ideology. Understandably for a work focused on Nazism and Protestantism, there is very little about what Nazi pagans sought to achieve. Despite a reference to Hitler's mockery of those who sought to revive the worship of ancient Teutonic gods (and, more surprisingly still, Rosenberg's declaration that Wotan was dead), what a belief system that rejected Christianity actually entailed remains unclear. That leading Nazis remained sympathetic to Protestantism has been richly demonstrated. But what the minority of Nazis who rejected Christianity believed is also important, and before we can be certain what to make of their pronouncements on Christ, we need to know better what they said about the faith that Christianity had bloodily displaced. As this book so well demonstrates, Nazism proved compatible with both Christianity and paganism. It shows, contrary to previous accounts, that the former was massively influential. But for a full sense of Nazism's religious landscape, we need to know more about the strand which argued not for the worship of an Aryan Christ but for the return of a belief in Valhalla.

Martin Durham
University of Wolverhampton

Ruan O'Donnell, *Robert Emmet and the Rebellion of 1798* (Irish Academic Press, Dublin, 2003) ISBN 0-7165-2788-X, 274pp., £39.50.

Ruan O'Donnell, *Robert Emmet and the Rising of 1803* (Irish Academic Press, Dublin, 2003) ISBN 0-7165-2786-3, 353pp., £39.50.

Marianne Elliott, *Robert Emmet: The Making of a Legend* (Profile Books, London, 2003) ISBN 1-867197-7, 292pp., £20.00.

Ruan O'Donnell is the author of two earlier volumes on the 1798 Rebellion and its aftermath in County Wicklow: *The Rebellion in Wicklow 1798* and *Aftermath: Post-Rebellion Insurgency in Wicklow 1799–1803*. These are both works of considerable scholarship and are essential reading for anyone interested in the United Irishmen and their attempts to throw off British rule. He is also the author of one of the best popular general accounts of the Rebellion, his *1798 Diary*, reprinted from articles originally published in the *Irish Times*. Given this track record, his study of Robert Emmet and the 1803 Rising was something very much to be looked forward to. The two volumes he has published exceed these expectations.

O'Donnell provides us with much more than just a biography of Robert Emmet, who was after all still in his twenties when executed. Instead we are provided with an outstanding contribution to the history of the Irish revolutionary movement, with Emmet's role being made a special point of focus. The first of the two volumes, on Emmet and 1798, makes an important contribution to the history of the United Irishmen, to the history of the Rebellion itself especially in Dublin, and to the relatively neglected history of the revolutionary movement's subsequent recovery. As O'Donnell shows, the revolutionary underground was not destroyed by the fearful bloodletting and brutal repression of 1798. Despite some 30,000 fatalities at the hands of the British and their Orange allies, despite thousands of imprisonments, transportions and conscriptions, despite widespread torture and summary execution, the movement survived. It was reorganised in 1799 and prepared itself for another attempt in 1803.

Far from being the daydream of an idealistic and naive young man, the 1803 attempt was, as O'Donnell shows in his second volume, the work of a revolutionary cadre, hardened by the experience of repression, and determined on a reckoning. O'Donnell not only provides by far the best biographical account of Emmet himself but more importantly he delineates his relations with this revolutionary cadre, rescuing from neglect and obscurity men of the stamp of Arthur Devlin, Malachy Delaney, Philip Rourke, William Dowdall, Philip Long and others. His scholarship and industry are to be wholeheartedly commended and serve to provide the reader with a street-level view of events as well as of the more elevated negotiations with the French.

How realistic were the prospects for success in 1803? With a French invasion, success would have seemed certain, although the rebels would have then been faced with the problem of their relations with Napoleon. Without the French or with the French only coming as reinforcements, there seems little doubt that Emmet's plan for the seizure of Dublin offered the best prospect for raising the country. Whether the North would have risen in such an event still needs further research, but there is every reason to believe that success in Dublin would have rallied the movement elsewhere. What prospect was there for success in Dublin? Certainly the rebels achieved virtually complete surprise. They laid their plans, perfected their organisation and successfully accumulated huge quantities of munitions in the city, including mines and rockets. The rockets would have substituted for artillery, the lack of which had seriously damaged the rebel cause in 1798. When the authorities searched the rebels' secret Marshal sea depot after the event they discovered 150,000 musket balls and 42,000 ball cartridges, more ammunition than the city yeomanry had available. Thousands of collapsible pikes were ready for distribution. What seems to have caused the attempt to misfire is the decision to stage the rising before there were firearms available. These were still in France, 4,000 muskets stockpiled at Rouen and Le Havre, but as O'Donnell observes, 'the hastily arranged uprising... left no time for organising a major gun-running operation'. The organisation included in its ranks professional smugglers more than capable of such an enterprise, but there was not the time. Once it became apparent that there were no firearms most of those committed to the cause either stayed at home or quickly dispersed. In the event, Emmet took to the streets with hundreds rather than thousands following him. The result was disaster. What is interesting, however, is that even after Emmet himself fled the scene, there remained others on the streets determined to strike a blow against the authorities regardless. Indeed, according to O'Donnell there were actually more men in arms after Emmet had fled than before. As he puts it, 'small bodies of pikemen and gunmen vented frustration at a regime which had flogged, imprisoned, shot and transported thousands of their comrades'. A night of skirmishing left perhaps fifty people dead, among them the Attorney General Lord Kilwarden, dragged from his coach and piked. Being a gentleman, historians routinely express sympathy for the 'humane' Kilwarden, but as O'Donnell points out, he had sentenced children to transportation and was implicated in the judicial murder of William Orr.

In the aftermath of the Rising, some 3,000 arrests were made and some thirty rebels, including Emmet, were eventually executed. The United Irishmen had finally been defeated. O'Donnell's conclusions sum it all up to good effect: the Rising has been generally underrated and it has been too much associated with Emmet rather than recognised as the work of an extensive revolutionary underground, made up of brave and determined men who deserve to be rescued from the condescension of posterity. This he has achieved.

While O'Donnell's contribution was something to look forward to with eager anticipation, Marianne Elliott's book aroused quite contrary expectations. An assault on the republican tradition is one of the hallmarks of her work and this volume does not disappoint. Her actual biographical account of Emmet, just under a hundred pages, is well worth reading, but when she gets on to an examination of 'the legend', her aims become clear. Of course, a good historian is not necessarily one you agree with, but one you learn from and are challenged by. Elliott signally fails to score in this respect with a tendentious survey that blames the tradition for the circumstances that sustained it rather than the other way round. Her point-scoring is a recurring irritation that can easily be turned against her. It is really not good enough, for example, to refer to the Easter Rising as causing 'appalling bloodshed' for which the republican tradition and the Emmet legend must bear responsibility without also acknowledging the responsibility that the Home Rule tradition had for the deaths of far, far greater numbers of Irishmen sent to die in the even more appalling blood-shed on the Western Front. A very strong, indeed I would argue, incontrovertible, case can be made that Pearse, Collins and co. actually saved the lives of a considerable number of young Irishmen by their opposition first to recruitment and later to conscription. The reason Marianne Elliott, Roy Foster and those of like mind do not acknowledge this is, of course, that the Western Front was the work of the properly constituted authorities.

John Newsinger
Bath Spa University College

John Callaghan, Steven Fielding and Steve Ludlam (eds), *Interpreting the Labour Party: Approaches to Labour politics and history* (Manchester University Press, Manchester, 2003), ISBN 0-7190-6718-9, 224pp., £45.

This collection of essays will not only be welcomed by university under-graduates looking for a guide to theories and accounts of the British Labour Party's evolution and character but should also revive and renew debates about the relative merits of different analyses and accounts of the party.

Nick Randall's essay reviewing explanations for the particular trajectory of the Labour Party provides a useful opening chapter, although he does rather shoehorn the various explanations into his five categories: material-ist, ideational, electoral, institutional and a fifth, synthetic, that combines and compresses some or all of the previous four. Randall introduces and con-textualises a number of debates that are treated in greater detail in subsequent chapters, in particular the debate about structure and agency that runs implicitly or explicitly throughout the volume. One ongoing debate con-cerns the centrality of electoral considerations to any analysis of Labour's programmatic trajectory. New Labour has operated a strategy clearly based more on preference accommodation than preference shaping (Iraq aside). How else is one to explain the centrality of the Gouldian focus group to New Labour strategy? Randall limits himself to warning that: 'Those minded to employ electoral verdicts as the basis for ideological revision therefore face untangling the contribution of ideological commitments from party campaigning, image, leadership and its capacity to counter attack its opponents.' It is a worthwhile project, and eminently more feasible than Randall suggests.

The electoral question is the central one in Steven Fielding and Declan McHugh's account of David Marquand's *The Progressive Dilemma*. The dilemma that Marquand highlighted was the inability of the Labour Party to stay in office, an inability he attributed to the party's too-close association with the manual working class and the trade unions. Tony Blair and those present at the creation of New Labour (Phillip Gould, for example) had clearly digested the Marquand message and, as Marquand himself conceded, to an extent have transcended the 'dilemma'.

Lawrence Black advances the discussion by looking at how the 'new political history' has raised questions relating to earlier studies of the party, arguing that 'the people' have often served as a brake on the radicalism of its leadership, and making the postwar British electorate sound like the inspiration for Marcuse's *One Dimensional Man*. Nevertheless, this is an interesting, at times provocative, essay and leads into the heart of the volume—a series of essays on key individuals who have offered accounts and critiques of the Labour Party. Alastair Reid attempts a reappraisal of the 'worthy but rather dull' Henry Pelling and John Callaghan dissects Ross McKibbin's studies of the origins and early evolution of the party and the centrality of working-class culture to any explanation of the form the party assumed, highlighting both discontinuities and silences in McKibbin's analysis.

The chapters by Madeleine Davis on New Left critiques of 'Labourism', by Michael Newman on Ralph Miliband and Mark Wickham-Jones on Tom Nairn, are all illuminating and overlapping pieces. Davis roots New Left critiques in the earlier work of Theodore Rothstein, who had posed the question of "Why is socialism in England at a discount?" as early as 1898, and found the answer in the specific nature of 'labourism'. As an account of the trajectory of New Left critiques, this is an excellent account, and contains such gems as a sample from the line of questioning Michael Foot faced when subjecting himself to a 1968 *New Left Review* interview ('young militants ask themselves today whether a struggle against the Labour party as it is might not eventually be an unavoidable form that the struggle for socialism must take at a time when the Labour government is actually the executor of British capitalism.') The key intellectual force behind New Left critiques was, of course, Ralph Miliband and here his biographer provides a clear and succinct account of Miliband's often misunderstood intention in writing *Parliamentary Socialism*. Not surprisingly, Miliband's disappointment, if that is not too light a word for it, at the Wilson governments' performance —particularly in relation to the Vietnam War—is emphasised, but it is also good to see a full account of the way in which Miliband somewhat revised his view of the potential inherent in the party during the early 1980s as he developed a close personal relationship with Tony Benn, whom he saw as a potential leader 'receptive to socialist ideas'. Arguably, David Coates and Leo Panitch should be the subject of chapters in this volume.

Effectively in writing a chapter about Milibandianism beyond Miliband, they have made themselves so, outlining the evolution of a Milibandian perspective to which they have been central, in particular by taking it into the arena of international and comparative political economy. One benefit of this has been to add a new dimension to studies of the contemporary Labour Party, so that 'when we came back to writing about New Labour, we were better situated to write about the Blairite economic project than were many of the scholars whose work had remained sharply focused on party politics and party issues alone.'

Beyond this, Steve Ludlam and Eric Shaw provide two chapters on the Labour Party-trade unions link. The former subjects to scrutiny both pluralist and marxist interpretations of the link, arguing that any analysis should 'avoid both monolithism, treating the unions as [Martin] Harrison's 'oparthodox lump of suet pudding', and bipolarism, treating the labour alliance as a simple combination of 'the unions' with 'the party', and instead should recognise the 'existence of virtually permanent crosscutting factionalism, in which individual unions take up opposing positions alongside distinct groups of party members and leaders'. Crucially, he ends by pointing to the difficulties that those researching in this area face. Eric Shaw provides what must be the most systematic consideration of Lewis Minkin's contribution to our understanding of the nature of the Labour Party to date, showing how Minkin's work demolished what Shaw calls the 'baronial power' thesis through his utilisation of role theory. He closes by raising key questions about the continued centrality of the link under New Labour, and of the continued relevance of Minkin's approach in the search for answers to them. The volume itself ends with Colin Hay, outlining theoretical and analytical issues involved in the study of the party, presenting issues that run throughout the volume, but this time situating them within the context and language of what he terms a 'new political science of British politics'. Whether this observation and cataloguing of trends adds up to anything as coherent as a 'new political science' is a separate question. If a volume of this nature, representing a range of viewpoints and approaches, did not generate a basis for keen discussion and even at times provoke the reader, it would have failed. This nicely balanced volume succeeds and should itself become a reference point for future studies of the Labour Party.

Mark Phythian
University of Wolverhampton

G. Lukacs, *A Defence of 'History and Class Consciousness'. Tailism and the Dialectic*, trans. E. Leslie (Verso, London & New York, 2002), ISBN 1-85984-370-0, 182pp., £10 pbk.

Few intellectual reputations have oscillated so wildly as that of Georg Lukacs. Relegated to the sidelines of official Marxist discourse, for the majority of his career—accorded only the most perfunctory of mentions in the *Great Soviet Encyclopedia* and completely ignored in the pages of Maurice Cornforth's masterly survey of *Communism and Philosophy*—he was rediscovered and whole-heartedly embraced by the student generation of the 1960s.[1] It was they who perceived in his work the nucleus of a 'Western Marxist' tradition, that was seemingly more potent, humanistic, and individualist than its Soviet counterpart, and which could be offered as an alternate road to socialism that was unscarred by memories of Stalin's labour camps, by the consolidation of Marx's writings into a rigid dogma, and by the compromises and failures inherent in the actual wielding of political power. Thus, Lukacs was feted as the 'leading Marxist intellectual' of the twentieth century, a solitary, enigmatic, and noble figure, who had championed the unity of art and politics in the fashioning of a revolutionary culture and systematically deployed his formidable intellect, for more than fifty years, in reasoning his way towards a new and inspiring future for all of humanity.

Yet, no sooner had his legacy been celebrated and his works—previously only available in obscure translations—been republished and widely discussed, than the collapse of the USSR and its satellites served to sweep the study of Marxism from the university curriculum, and to fatally expose the shallow and insubstantial roots set down by 'Western Marxism' in both the union movement and an increasingly fragmented and demoralised left. In this period of general reaction, Lukacs now came to represent all that had been worst about existing socialism. He was the intellectual who had buckled under the encroaching power of Stalinism, an 'accomplished groveller', who had tailored his thoughts to suit each new expediency, expunging and repudiating his earlier writings wholesale, at the will of a succession of authoritarian task masters: Zinoviev, Stalin, Rakosi, and Kadar.[2]

In such circumstances, the sweeping vision and augmentative force of his ideas were first obscured and then completely obliterated by his constant trimming, and by the erasing of abandoned positions and uncomfortable thoughts from the canon of his work. Thus, any claims to a grand theoretical scheme with which to revitalise an ailing Marxism were lost beneath the sheer weight of his remaining sorry and spurned palimpsests, and his abject recantation of his seminal contribution to political theory, *History and Class*

Consciousness. However, it would appear from a manuscript discovered in the vaults of the former Marx-Lenin Institute in Moscow—and published here, for the first time, as *A Defence of History and Class Consciousness*—that Lukacs was far more spirited and tenacious in combating his critics, in both the fractured Hungarian Communist Party and the increasingly centralising Comintern hierarchy, than had ever previously been thought to be the case.

Writing as an exile, in Vienna, in 1925–26, Lukacs still enjoyed considerable prestige in the international communist movement. Having distinguished himself as a political commissar and as the minister for culture in Bela Kun's short-lived Soviet government, he had been at the forefront of decision-making throughout the Hungarian revolution and had tasted action on more than one occasion. Moreover, when the gunfire had finally subsided over Bucharest and a grim reaction triumphed, he had not retreated back into his study in order to distance himself from the struggle or to exonerate himself from the blame of the defeat. Rather, he attempted to provide a thoroughgoing analysis of the reasons behind the collapse of the revolutionary movement across Central and Eastern Europe, from 1918–22, that was intended to provide a blueprint for future success and to establish himself, alongside Lenin and Luxemburg, as one of the chief intellectual exponents of a new, militant and insurrectionary brand of Marxism.

The full extent of his ambition was evident in the text of *History and Class Consciousness*, which—based upon a series of articles written between 1919 and 1922—was published by an avant-garde German printing house in the spring of 1923, and provoked storms of criticism and choruses of praise in roughly equal measure. This is hardly surprising for, unencumbered by a sense of intellectual modesty or respect for the intellectual reputations of others, Lukacs sought to continue and fully develop Marx's study of alienation—or 'reification' as he now styled it—from precisely where the old master had left off. In such, he was both remarkably successful in re-establishing a current of idealism within Marxism, and amazingly prescient in emphasising the enormity of the young Marx's debt to Hegelian philosophy. Subsequently, reinforced by the discovery and publication of Marx's *Economic and Philosophical Manuscripts* of 1844, Lukacs plausibly advanced the view that alienation was at the very heart of that philosopher's critique of capitalism, with technology and morality diverging ever more sharply with the onset of industrialisation, and a clear distinction becoming evident between Marx's Hegelian, humanistic roots, and Engels's supposedly dour materialism and all-too trusting belief in the liberating potentials of manufacture and science. In seeking to drive a wedge between Marx and Engels, Lukacs was not only providing potent ammunition for a future generation of Cold War scholars, but was also far exceeding his stated brief in reclaiming the Hegelian influences upon Marxist philosophy. He was, instead, attempting to radically recast Marx as a Hegelian—first and foremost—and to set his theories firmly within the context of the German Romantic and anti-scientific movement.

Consequently, for Lukacs, it was human consciousness, rather than just a matter of class or economics, which provided the driving motor for contemporary history and which was to be the decisive factor in the coming proletarian revolution. The seizure of the state apparatus was, he held, not enough to ensure the maintenance of Soviet power, if the proletariat had not first won the ideological battle, dissolving both the cultural and intellectual bonds of capitalism and attaining communism through participation in a struggle which, by its very nature, would ensure their attainment of a true and lasting class consciousness. Unfortunately, with the Soviet Union ringed by hostile powers, and the revolutionary movement comprehensively defeated not only in Hungary, but also in Germany, Austria, Bulgaria, and Finland, Lukacs's belief in the eventual triumph of a new, socialist, man seemed spectacularly misplaced and the product of a near-mystical faith, rather than any hard reasoning. Worse still, it was his rival within the Hungarian party—the irascible and proudly anti-intellectual Bela Kun—who had the ear of Zinoviev, prior to his convening of the Fifth Congress of the Comintern, in June 1924, and who co-ordinated the attacks that threatened to swamp Lukacs on the floor of the meeting. Thus, while Kun's new disciple Lazslo Rudas—together with Abram Deborin, one of the foremost Soviet philosophers of the period—penned detailed critiques of his work, Zinoviev thundered against it from the presidium, loudly proclaiming that: 'If we get a few more of these professors [such as Lukacs] spinning their Marxist theories we shall be lost!'

However, though his masterpiece had been judged and found wanting, Lukacs did not immediately seek an accommodation with his powerful detractors, but instead immediately set to work producing a *Defence* of his writings, which was designed to reassert his own claims to Marxist orthodoxy and debt to Leninism. The resulting manuscript, written in haste, left unfinished, and never subsequently alluded to by Lukacs anywhere in his voluminous public and private pronouncements, is—by its very nature—unpolished, scrappy, and extremely harsh in its polemical tone. Yet it is also direct and benefits from a certain immediacy and liveliness that is not always to be found in Lukacs's later, and more carefully considered, theoretical writings. Moreover, the potential difficulty for a contemporary readership in appraising a text that was designed purely to settle an academic controversy that raged some eighty years ago, is more than resolved by the two very different essays that pre- and post-face Lukacs's short study.

For John Rees—in a thoughtful and very well researched piece—the youthful Lukacs is a tragic hero, to be embraced by one particular branch of the Trotskyite movement as a forceful opponent of the encroaching power of Stalinism who was capable of charting an attractive alternate course in the history of the Third International, and who was representative of an authentic Leninist strain within Bolshevism that was thoroughly at odds with the accretions later foisted upon it by Zinoviev and his allies. Conversely, for Slavoj Zizek—whose essay concludes the volume—Lukacs's ideas reflected a clear break with Leninist practice and prefigured the existential Marxism of Sartre and his own *Praxis* group of Yugoslav philosophers in the 1960s. Though perhaps we learn far more from Zizek about himself and the fate of contemporary Marxism in the Balkans than we ever do about Lukacs's own theoretical contributions to the science in the mid-1920s, his article is both starkly poignant and beautifully written, evoking a host of lost opportunities for the movement and bitterly mourning both the break-up of the Yugoslav Federation and the criminal waste of Evald Ilyenkov's genius, as the last great Soviet philosopher.

That both viewpoints are, to an extent, justifiable through an examination of Lukacs's work testifies not only to the purposeful ambiguity of his position in 1924–25, but also to the continuing richness of the competing currents within modern-day Marxism. This said, there can be little doubt that Lukacs's *Defence* was attempting a stubborn rearguard action against the author's influential detractors, while constantly introducing fresh ideas to the argument under the guise of conventional Marxist orthodoxy. The problem for Lukacs, and which eventually led to the compromising of both his work and reputation, was that this approach simply left far too many hostages to fortune.

As before, he was dismissive of the primacy of economics, dismissing the work of his critics as degenerating 'into vulgar bourgeois economics' of the type of Kautsky and Hilferding (p.113), before—after some initial uncertainty—marshalling all of his forces against Engels's view of historical materialism (p.119). For Lukacs, there were no dialectics in external nature and the theoretical flaws—introduced into the Marxist system by Engels during 'a ripe old age'—'enthusiastically multiply, and are raised up into the system…for the purposes of liquidating' the critical apparatus of the science (pp.136–7). Marx, in overturning Hegelian philosophy had—it was argued—'rescued its real core', and it was precisely this that Lukacs now aimed to salvage from the dangerous legacy unwittingly bequeathed by Engels to the more malevolent of his disciples, such as Deborin and Rudas. Marx, and by extension Hegel were, therefore, now to be reclaimed for an intellectually rigorous form of idealism, with all truth being seen as relative to the standpoint of individual classes and the universal spirit being realised by the role of the communist party, which would bring the proletariat to embrace and effect the power of their own consciousness, in sweeping away the last vestiges of inequality and conflict from the face of the world.

Yet, in arguing that the social was also spiritual, Lukacs did not stint upon using invective, attacking Rudas's 'exact' and 'scientific' soul, casting Deborin—rather than himself—as an unreconstructed Hegelian—and damning both 'the open Menshevism of Deborin and tail-ending of Rudas' as typifying everything that was wrong with the revolutionary movement and which had retarded, so disastrously, the export of Bolshevism to Hungary. It was perhaps this intemperance, and a realisation that the resolution of conflicting theories was increasingly coming to be played out in the cellars of the Lubianka, rather than in the plush surroundings of lecture and conference halls, that led Lukacs to shelve his plans to publish his *Defence* and to carry his knowledge of its existence with him to the grave. However, in composing the work, and in producing *Lenin. A Study of the Unity of his Thought* (Vienna, 1924, rpt. London, 1970)—which was widely disseminated at precisely the same time—he had shown no inclination either to abandon his original ambition to stand at the intellectual forefront of the communist movement, or to refrain from explicitly citing both Marx and Lenin as final arbiters in all questions of theoretical debate.

Given that Lenin had spoken dismissively of his intellectual abilities, his failure to support his political theories with solid evidence, and his 'purely verbal' commitment to Marxism, Lukacs quickly and predictably found himself to be on extremely difficult ground.[3] Moreover, having stripped away all that is brutally practical in the struggle for power—the strikes, riots, imprisonments and civil wars that accompanied revolutionary action—he appeared to overlook the uncomfortable fact that reality is not so easily given to command, or to order, as an abstract theory. 'Western Marxism', limited to a theorising perspective without an accompanying social movement, was thus as ill-equipped to survive the crises and bloodshed of the 1920s and 1930s as was the collapse of existing socialism after 1989. Moreover, though the publication of this remarkable manuscript testifies that Lukacs was neither as spineless nor as vacillating as had once been thought, it was to be his personal tragedy—and that of European Marxism as a whole—that having initially appealed for a definitive synthesis of Marxism-Leninism, it was to be Stalin's vision, rather than his own, that was to be durable and plausible enough to prevail, once a ring of steel closed about the Soviet Union and fascism began to stalk the corners of the globe. Only then, as a prisoner of his own logic and unwilling to either apostatise his communism, or forsake the working class, did Lukacs seek to bend the knee and repudiate his great writings. In a gentler age for European scholars, where adherence to ideology does not automatically carry with it the threat of exile, imprisonment and death, we would be mistaken to condemn Georg Lukacs too harshly. Against the backdrop of the ruins of his utopian dreams, in the very midst of counter-revolutionary terror, victorious fascism, and total war, he—like the Abbé de Sieyes before him—could at least say that he had survived, and that his voice—if dimmed—had not completely ceased in speaking out for the cause of the poor and dispossessed.

John Callow
Goldsmiths College, University of London

Notes

1. A. M. Prokhorov (ed. in chief), *Great Soviet Encyclopedia*, 3rd edition (Moscow & London, 1974), vol.15, pp.170–1; M. Cornforth, *Communism and Philosophy. Contemporary dogmas and revisions of Marxism* (London, 1980).
2. A. Kadarkay, *Georg Lukacs: Life, Thought, and Politics* (Oxford, 1991), pp.xi & 3; T. Eagleton, 'Kettles Boil, Classes Struggle', *London Review of Books*, (20 February 2003), p.18.
3. V. I. Lenin, 'On the Question of Parliamentarianism' in *Collected Works* (Moscow, 1966), vol.31, p.165.